Edward Payson Crowell, Henry Bullard Richardson

A Brief History of Roman Literature for Schools and Colleges

Edward Payson Crowell, Henry Bullard Richardson

A Brief History of Roman Literature for Schools and Colleges

ISBN/EAN: 9783744782111

Printed in Europe, USA, Canada, Australia, Japan

Cover: Foto ©Paul-Georg Meister /pixelio.de

More available books at **www.hansebooks.com**

A BRIEF HISTORY

OF

ROMAN LITERATURE

FOR

SCHOOLS AND COLLEGES.

TRANSLATED AND EDITED FROM THE GERMAN OF
HERMANN BENDER

BY

E. P. CROWELL AND H. B. RICHARDSON,
PROFESSORS OF LATIN IN AMHERST COLLEGE.

GINN & COMPANY
BOSTON · NEW YORK · CHICAGO · LONDON

Entered according to Act of Congress, in the year 1879, by
H. B. RICHARDSON,
In the Office of the Librarian of Congress, at Washington

88.2

The Athenæum Press
GINN & COMPANY · PROPRIETORS · BOSTON · U.S.A.

AUTHOR'S PREFACE.

THE present Outline History of Roman Literature is specially designed to meet the wants of schools. It is intended primarily to contain what a gymnasium student needs to know, and at the same time all such material taken from Roman literary history as can well be employed in Gymnasium instruction. For this reason, completeness of treatment has from the outset not been designed. On the other hand, I trust I have not omitted anything essential to the purpose already stated. In respect to form, I have had in view brevity and compactness of statement, together with the greatest possible comprehensiveness and precision.

As regards the arrangement of the work, I have in the main, within the separate periods, followed the principle of division according to topics, yet it has not seemed to me expedient to preserve entire consistency on this point in the case of those poets and prose-writers who have been active in more than one department. I have preferred, in each case, to give the full treatment of these writers under the head of that department in which they were most important; for example, Cicero under the head of Oratory. This inconsistency, by means of which a connected and complete view of such literary phenomena is gained, seems to me justifiable.

It will not be required of a teacher, who prepares a work like the present, that he shall have made special investigations in every direction. What may properly be demanded is, that he show thorough knowledge of the literature itself,— not merely of school literature,— and independent judgment. I trust that these necessary requisitions have been met.

The accompanying tables contain all the names cited in the text.

In the preparation of the work I have received very kind assistance from my honored teacher, Professor Dr. von Teuffel, of the University in this place, not only through the abundant information drawn from his History of Roman Literature, but also through personal advice, for which I herewith express to him my most heartfelt thanks.

H. BENDER.

TÜBINGEN, April, 1876.

TRANSLATOR'S PREFACE.

THE favorable reception given to Professor Hermann Bender's "Grundriss der Römischen Literaturgeschichte," published a few years since in Germany, and its extensive adoption as a text-book in the secondary schools of that country, suggested its translation for the use of schools and colleges in America.

The author enjoyed peculiar advantages in the preparation of the work, from the fact that he was a pupil of the late Professor Dr. Teuffel, of the University of Tübingen, the celebrated author of a complete History of Roman Literature, lately made accessible to English scholars in a translation.

In preparing the present manual, the aim has been to faithfully reproduce the original, both in subject-matter and form, with only such slight changes and omissions as seemed to be demanded for clearness of expression.

For the convenience of teachers and students, numerous references have been made to the best English works on Roman Literature, and also to valuable treatises on particular authors.

The somewhat meager table of contents has been greatly enlarged, so as to furnish a complete analysis of the work. Also the charts at the end have been thrown into much more convenient form than in the German edition.

It is hoped that the work, as thus constituted, will meet a want, long felt by classical teachers, of a text-book on Roman Literature, which should contain, in compact and convenient form, what every student ought to know, and which at the same time should serve as a basis for courses of lectures or for more extended study.

No reference has been made to American editions of Latin authors, since it has been taken for granted that teachers are well acquainted with them. For a complete bibliography of Latin Literature, teachers are referred to the admirable work of Professor Mayor, published by Macmillan & Co.

Special acknowledgements are due to Mr. G. H. Stockbridge, late of the University of Leipzig, for very valuable assistance in the work of translation and in the revision of the proof-sheets, and also to Mr. W. G. Hale, Tutor in Harvard University, for many timely suggestions.

AMHERST COLLEGE,
 Dec. 29, 1879.

PREFACE TO THE SECOND EDITION.

THE changes in the present edition consist mainly in the insertion of the Author's Preface, the recasting of certain paragraphs, and the correction of a few typographical errors.

AMHERST, March, 1880.

ABBREVIATIONS.

C.—Cruttwell's History of Roman Literature.
Con.—Conington's Miscellaneous Writings.
Dict. Antiqq.—Smith's Dictionary of Greek and Roman Antiquities.
Mer.—Merivale's History of the Romans under the Empire.
Mom.—Mommsen's History of Rome.
Parry.—Parry's Commentary on Terence.
Pn.—Papillon's Comparative Philology applied to Latin and Greek Inflections.
R.—Roby's Grammar of the Latin Language.
Ry.—Ramsay's Roman Antiquities.
S.—Sellar's Roman poets of the Republic.
T.—Teuffel's History of Roman Literature, translated by Wagner.
W.—Wordsworth's Fragments and Specimens of Early Latin.
Wh.—Whitney's Language and the Study of Language.

ANALYSIS.

INTRODUCTION.

1. Late development of Roman
 Literature 1
 Character of the Romans . . 1
 Their lack of imagination . . 1
 Their practical tendency . . 1
 Comparison with the Greeks . 1
 Attitude of contempt towards
 Greek culture 1
 Want of time for literary pur-
 suits 1
 Character of Roman Litera-
 ture in the first five centuries 2
 Comparatively late develop-
 ment of poetry 2
 Lack of a native Heroic Epos;
 the reason for this 2

Need of an impulse from with-
 out 2
 Indebtedness of Roman Liter-
 ature to the Greek 2
 Gradual advance of Greek
 ideas 2
2. The Italic language 3
 The Latin language 3
 The Alphabet 3
 Slow development of the lan-
 guage 3
 Influence of Ennius and Cicero 4
 Special adaptation to prose . 4
 Characteristics of the Latin . 4
 Stages of its decline 4
3. Periods of Roman Literature 5

FIRST PERIOD.

PRE-HISTORIC TO 240 B.C.

Struggle for political supremacy 7
Independent development of the
 Romans 7
The practical direction of prose
 and poetry 7
Character of archaic Latin . . 8
Literary barrenness of this period 8

I. Poetry.

Lack of a national Epos . . . 8
Niebuhr's theory refuted . . . 8
The Carmen. Versus Saturnius 8
Songs on historical subjects . . 8

Hymns to the dead 9
Carmina triumphalia 9
Sacred songs 9
 Carmen Saliare, Carmen Ar-
 valium 9
Ritual precepts 9
Epitaphs 9
The Drama 9
 Its origin 10
 Fescennini 10
 Satura 10
 Atellana 10
 Rude character of the above . . 11

II. Prose.

Crude and fragmentary nature of early prose 11
Conservative spirit of the Romans 11
Official Documents:
   Treaties 11
   Leges regiae 12
   Commentarii regum 12
   Commentarii magistratuum . 12
   Libri magistratuum 12

Priestly Literature:
   Libri pontificum 12
   Commentarii pontificum . . 12
   Fasti 12
   Annales pontificum 12
   Private chronicles 13
   Laudationes funebres . . . 13
   Leges XII Tabularum . . . 13
   Ius Flavianum 13
First prose-writer:
   Ap. Claudius Caecus 13

SECOND PERIOD.

FROM LIVIUS ANDRONICUS TO CICERO, 240–70 B.C.

General character 14
Growing influence of Greek culture 14
Causes contributing to it . . 15
Opposition to it unsuccessful . 15
Its restriction to the aristocracy 15
Growing unpopularity of the national writers 15
Influence of Ennius 15
Prominence of comedy . . . 15
Beginnings of oratory, history, and legal writings 16

I. Poetry.

a.—The Drama.

The national popular comedy.
   Satura and Atellana 16
   Chief representatives:
     Novius 16
     L. Pomponius 16
   Popular character of comedy 16
The Hellenistic Drama.
   The Roman Theatre 17
   Unpopularity of the actor's profession 17
   Classes appealed to by the drama 17

Hellenistic comedy.
   Fabula palliata 17
   Its prototypes 17
   Its general character . . . 17
   Scene of the palliata . . . 18
   Different varieties 18
   Combination of two or more plays 18
   Chief representatives:
     Livius Andronicus . . . 18
     Ennius 18
     Cn. Naevius 18
     T. Maccius Plautus . . . 19
       His life and extant writings 19
       Characterization of Plautus 20
       His wit and vivacity . . 20
       Character of his verse . . 20
       His fame in later times . 20
     P. Terentius 20
       His life and writings . . 20
       Comparison between Terence and Plautus . . . 21
       His defects and excellences 21
       Elegance and dignity of his language 21
       His fame 21

ANALYSIS.

Statius Cæcilius 21
Luscius Lavinius 21
The National Drama.
Fabula togata 22
Its general character . . . 22
Chief authors:
  Titinius 22
  T. Quinctius Atta 22
  L. Afranius 22
Tragedy.
Hellenistic tendency 22
Comparatively slight cultivation 22
Faults of the Roman tragic writers 22
Fabula prætexta 22
Chief authors:
  Livius Andronicus. . . . 22
  Cn. Nævius 22
  Q. Ennius. 22
  M. Pacuvius 22
  L. Accius 23

b.—The Epos.

Its character 23
Chief authors:
  Livius Andronicus 23
  Cn. Nævius 24
  Q. Ennius 24
    His life and chief work . . 24
    Character of the Annales . 24
    Use of the hexameter . . 24
    Genius of Ennius 25
    His work a great national Epos 25
    His estimation in later times 25
Satura; its new meaning . . . 25
Chief representative:
  C. Lucilius 25
    His life 25
    His sharp criticism of public affairs 25

II. Prose.

General character rude and undeveloped 26
Comparison with early German prose 26

a.—History.

Annalistic character 26
Discussion of its trustworthiness 26
Writers in Greek:
  Q. Fabius Pictor 26
  L. Cincius Alimentus . . . 27
  C. Acilius Glabrio 27
  A. Postumius Albinus . . . 27
Latin writers:
  M. Porcius Cato 27
    His life and character . . 27
    His versatility 27
    The Origines 27
    Character of the narrative . 27
    Introduction of speeches . 28
    Cato's authorities . . . 28
    Cicero's estimate of him . 28
  Cassius Hemina 28
  L. Calpurnius Piso Frugi . . 28
  C. Sempronius Tuditanus . . 28
  L. Cælius Antipater 28
Writers of contemporary history:
  P. Rutilius Rufus 28
  Q. Lutatius Catulus 28
  Sempronius Asellio 28
  L. Cornelius Sulla 28
  L. Cornelius Sisenna . . . 29
  Claudius Quadrigarius . . . 29
  Valerias Antias 29
  C. Licinius Macer 29

b.—Oratory.

Favored by the character of the Romans, and by the freedom of their political life 29

Necessity to the political aspirant	29
Cicero's requirements for the orator	30
Most important orators:	
M. Porcius Cato	30
S. Sulpicius Galba	30
C. Gracchus	30
M. Antonius	30
L. Crassus	30
Q. Hortensius	30
Rhetorica ad Herennium	31
Cornificius	31

c.—Special Sciences.

Jurisprudence	31
Development of Roman law normal	31
Beginnings of legal science	31
Legal tradition in certain families	31
Chief writers:	
S. Ælius Pætus	31
P. Mucius Scævola	32
Q. Mucius Scævola	32
Archæology	32
Chiefly occupied with linguistic matters	32
Zealous pursuit of philological studies	32
First Roman philologist:	
L. Ælius Stilo	32
Domestic Economy and Agriculture	33
Cato	33
Mago	33
Condition of other sciences	33

THIRD PERIOD.

Golden Age of Roman Literature, 70 B.C.–14 A.D.

Predominance of Greek culture	34
Roman students in Greece	34
Greek teachers in Rome	34
Contempt for the Greeks	34
Real dependence upon them	34
Translation of Greek works in the schools	34
Development of the book-trade	34
Founding of public libraries	35
Consequent increase of literary activity	35
Diverse character of the Ciceronian and Augustan Ages	35
Freedom of literature under the Republic	35
Its restraint under the Empire	36
Withdrawal of poetry to the court	36
Importance of oratory in the Ciceronian Age	36
Its highest development in Cicero	36
Cultivation of rhetoric, history, and philosophy	36
Comparative unimportance of poetry	36
Diplomatic character of literature under the Empire	36
Supression of individuality	36
Cautious treatment of oratory and history	36
Prominence of the professions	37
Courtly tone of poetry	37
Increased attention to literature in the provinces	37
None of the great Augustan authors native Romans	37

I. Poetry.
a.—The Drama.

The artistic drama little cultivated	38
Its restriction to limited circles	38

Its retreat before the Mime and
   Pantomime 38
The Mime: its character and
   subjects 38
Chief representatives:
   Decimus Laberius 39
   Publilius Syrus 39
The Pantomime:
   Its development by Bathyllus
   and Pylades 39
   Its general character . . . 39

b.— The Epos.

Its extensive cultivation . . . 39
Its varieties 39
Chief representatives:
   Cicero 40
   P. Terentius Varro 40
   L. Varius 40
   Pedo Albinovanus 40
   Rabirius 40
   Lucretius Carus 40
      His didactic poem *de rerum
      natura* 40
      The poet's purpose . . . 40
      His difficulties and success 41
      His literary importance . . 41
   P. Vergilius Maro 41
      His life and character . 41–42
      Order of his poems . . . 42
   1. Bucolica 42
      Their character and fame . 42
   2. Georgica 43
      Their subject 43
      Aim of the poet 43
      Degree of independence . 43
      Their general character . . 43
   3. Æneis 43
      Subject of the poem . . . 44
      Virgil's purpose 44
      Defects of the poem . . . 44
      Its finest parts 44
      Its great fame 44

Minor poems of Virgil 45
Virgil in the Middle Ages . . 45
Gratius Faliscus 45
Manilius 45

c.— Satire and Epistle.

Character of the satire 45
Its poetic form 45
Deviation from this form by
   Varro 45
Q. Horatius Flaccus 46
   His life 46
   Description of his person . . 46
   Varieties of his poems . . . 47
   Probable order of publication 47
1. Satires 47
   Varied character of their
      contents 47
   Their careless style . . . 48
   Their effect upon the reader 48
2. Epistles 48
   Their beauty of style . . . 48
   Questions discussed in them 48
   The finest ones 48
3. Odes 49
   Their time of publication . 49
   Imitation of Greek poets . 49
   Growing independence of
      Horace 49
   Reflective character of the
      odes 49
   Their beauty of thought and
      expression 50
4. Epodes 50
   Their relation to the odes
      and satires 50
   Subjects of the epodes . . 50
General estimate of Horace . . 50
   Reflective cast of his mind . 50
   His sound common sense . . 50
   His aim 50
   His independence in social
      relations 50

His importance as a poet . . 51
Comparison between Horace
   and Virgil. 51

d.— Lyric Poetry.

Its growth in importance 52
Copying the elegy from the
   Alexandrian poets 52
Introduction of the erotic elegy
   by Catullus 52
General character 52
Lyric poets of the Ciceronian
   Age :
   C. Licinius Calvus 52
   C. Valerius Catullus 52
      His life 52
      Subjects of his poems . . 52
      Character as a poet . . . 53
Lyric poets under Augustus :
   Cornelius Gallus 53
   P. Ovidius Naso 53
      His life in Rome 53
      Banishment by Augustus . . 53
      Cause assigned by Ovid . . 54
      His writings 54
      His facility in versification . 55
      Lack of earnestness . . . 55
      Comparison with the Ger-
         man poet Heine . . . 56
      Superficiality of Ovid's po-
         etry 56
      Popularity of the Metamor-
         phoses in the Middle Ages 56
   Albius Tibullus 56
      His life and writings . . . 56
      His elegiac nature 57
   S. Propertius 57
      Subjects of his poems . . 57
      Cultivation of the erotic
         elegy 57
      Smoothness and finish of
         his poetry 58
Quintilian on the Roman elegy . 58

II. Prose.
a.— Oratory.

The genus Asiaticum 58
The genus Atticum 58
The genus Rhodium 58
Their most prominent repre-
   sentatives 58
Restriction of oratory in the
   Augustan Age 58
Supplanted by Rhetoric . . . 58
Oratory of the schools 59
Orators of the Ciceronian Age :
   Caesar 59
   M. Calidius 59
   C. Mummius 59
   C. Curio 59
   M. Caelius Rufus 59
   Asinius Pollio 59
   M. Valerius Messala 59
Chief representative in the Au-
   gustan Age :
   Cassius Severus 59
Quintilian's characterization of
   these orators 59
   M. Tullius Cicero 59
      Survey of his life and writ-
         ings 59–61
      His activity in different de-
         partments 61
   1. Orations 62
      Quintilian's judgment of
         Cicero as an orator . . 62
      Cicero's oratorical endow-
         ments 62
      His zeal for knowledge . . 62
      Character of his orations . 62
      Most important ones . . 62–63
   2. Rhetorical writings 63
      Cicero's acquaintance with
         the theories of the schools 63
      His dissatisfaction with
         them 63

Practical nature of his own
   system 63
His rhetorical works in detail 64

b.—Cicero and Philosophy in Rome.

Unfriendly reception of Greek
   philosophy by the Romans . 64
Expulsion of Greek philosophers
   from Rome 64
Later popularity of Greek phil-
   osophy 65
Predominance of Stoicism . . 65
The different systems, with their
   representatives 65
Dependence of the Romans in
   philosophy 65
Constraint of Cicero's political
   life 65
His wide but superficial ac-
   quaintance with the Greek
   philosophers 66
His preference for the New
   Academy 66
His hostility to Epicureanism . 66
Cicero's chief service 66
Form of his writings 66
List of his philosophical works . 66

c.—Cicero's Letters.

The four collections 68
Their publication by Tiro and
   Atticus 69
General character of the letters 69
Their value as an historical
   authority 69
The diverse nature of the let-
   ters 69
Description of the collections . 70
Popularity of Cicero's letters in
   antiquity 70
General criticism of Cicero . . 70

Existing spirit of hypercriticism 70
Defects of Cicero's character . 71
His historical significance . . 71
Virtues and services of Cicero . 71

d.—History.

Activity in this department . . 72
Artistic treatment of history . . 72
The writers chiefly men en-
   gaged in politics 72
Diversity of subjects in the Cice-
   ronian and Augustan Age . 72
Writers of the Ciceronian Age:
   T. Pomponius Atticus . . . 72
   M. Tullius Cicero 72
   Q. Ælius Tubero 72
   C. Iulius Cæsar 73
      His life 73
      His position as an orator . 73
      Works on various subjects . 73
      His most important works . 73
      Survey of their contents . . 73
      General characterization of
         Cæsar 74
      His literary style 74
      His motives in writing . . 74
Continuation of Cæsar's his-
   tories by Aulus Hirtius . . 75
Cornelius Nepos 75
   His life and writings . . . 75
   His purpose in writing . . 76
   His sincerity and aim at im-
     partiality 76
   Defects of his works . . . 76
   Theory to account for them 76
C. Sallustius Crispus . . . 76
   His life and chief writings . 76
   1. Catilina 77
     Most interesting portions 77
   2. Bellum Iugurthinum . . . 77
     Its general character . . 77
   3. Historiæ 77

Martial's judgment of Sallust	77
Sallust's historical insight	78
Contrast between his life and his writings	78
His impartiality	78
His strength and his weakness	78
Peculiarities of his language	78
Writers of the Augustan Age:	
Augustus	78
M. Vipsanius Agrippa	79
M. Valerius Messala	79
Asinius Pollio	79
T. Livius	79
His life and writings	79
His aim in writing history	79
Livy's qualities of mind	80
Judgment of the ancients concerning him	80
His stand in religion and politics	80
Defects of his work	80
His authorities	81
Excellences of his work	81
His popularity	81
Pompeius Trogus	82
Iustinus	82
The *acta senatus* and *acta populi*	82

c.— Special Sciences.

M. Terentius Varro	82
His life and learning	82
The scope of his works	83
List of his most important works	83
General criticism	83
Value of Varro's works	84
S. Sulpicius Rufus	84
A. Ofilius	84
C. Trebatius Testa	84
M. Antistius Labeo	84
C. Ateius Capito	84
Writers on Archæology and Philology:	
P. Nigidius Figulus	84
M. Verrius Flaccus	84
Pompeius Festus	84
Iulius Hyginus	85
Architecture	85
Vitruvius Pollio	85
Geography	85
Agrippa	85

FOURTH PERIOD.

The Silver Age of Roman Literature, 14–117 A.D., from Tiberius to the Death of Trajan.

Imperial despotism unfavorable to literature	86
Suppression of freedom in speaking and writing	86
Consequent insincerity	86
Character of the language	87
Changes in style	87
Influences favorable to literature	87
Prominence of poetry and rhetoric	88
Learned character of the former	88
Predominance of the Epos	88
Its cultivation by the emperors	88
Its artificiality	88
School oratory and learning	88
History still under constraint	88
Literary importance of Spain and Gaul	89

I. Poetry.

a.—The Drama.

Predominance of the Mime and Pantomime	89
Absence of acting dramas	89
Tragic poets:	
Pomponius Secundus	89
Curiatius Maternus	89
Seneca	89
His ten tragedies	89
Their authenticity	89
French imitators of Seneca	90
Lucanus	90

b.—The Epos.

Nero	90
M. Annæus Lucanus	90
His life and writings	90
His poem, Pharsalia	90
His republican bias	90
His Stoicism	91
General character of his works	91
C. Valerius Flaccus	91
C. Silius Italicus	91
His life and writings	91
C. Papinius Statius	91
Character of his poems	92
The Silvæ	92
Writers of Didactic Epos:	
Germanicus	92
Cæsius Bassus	92
Lucilius Iunior	92

c.—Satire and Fable.

Abundance of materials for Satire	92
Its restriction to literary and social matters	93
Crabbedness of its tone	93
Its chief representatives	93
A. Persius Flaccus	93
Nature of his satires	93
Seneca	93
His attack on the emperor Claudius	93
Petronius Arbiter	94
His satirical romance	94
Abstract of the story	94
Its coarseness and wit	94
Question of identity discussed	94
Decimus Iunius Iuvenalis	95
Subjects of his satires	95
Their origin	95
His views on mankind and religion	95
His power of vivid portrayal	95
Languidness of his later satires	95
The most interesting satires	96
The Fable:	
Phædrus	96
His fables	96
Aim of the poet	96

d.—Lyric Poetry and Epigram.

Artificiality of Lyric Poetry	96
Cæsius Bassus	97
Statius	97
Aruntius Stella	97
Sulpicia	97
The Epigram	97
M. Valerius Martialis	97
His life	97
Character of his epigrams	97
His excellences	97
Lessing's estimate of him	97
His defects	97

II. Prose.

a.—History.

Suppression of free thought	98
Fate of A. Cremutius Cordus	98

Writers on contemporary history:
- Augustus 98
- Tiberius 98
- Claudius 98
- Agrippina the Younger . . . 99
- Vespasian 99
- Aufidius Bassus 99
- Pliny the Elder 99
- Fabius Rusticus 99
- Cluvius Rufus 99
- Velleius Paterculus 99
  - His life and writings . . . 99
  - His summary treatment of the earliest history . . . 99
  - Diffuseness of the latter part of his work 99
  - Its subjective character . . 99
  - Its artificial style 99
  - Excellences of the work . . 99
- Valerius Maximus 100
  - His collection of models for rhetoricians 100
  - Arrangement of the work . 100
  - The absurdity of its style . 100
  - Its value as a compilation . 100
- Q. Curtius Rufus 100
  - His history of Alexander the Great 100
  - General belief respecting the time of writing 100
  - Defects of the work . . . 100
  - The author's purpose . . . 100
  - His imitation of Livy . . . 101
  - His skill in dramatic grouping 101
- Cornelius Tacitus 101
  - Discussion respecting the place of his birth . . . 101
  - His life and writings . . . 101
  1. Dialogus de oratoribus . . 101
     - General character . . . 101
     - Discusssion of its authenticity 102
  2. De vita et moribus Iulii Agricolæ 102
     - General character . . . 102
  3. Germania 102
     - The monographic character of the work . . . 102
     - Its satirical purpose . . 102
  4. Historiæ 102
     - Most interesting portions 103
     - Time of composition . . 103
  5. Annales 103
     - Its relation to the Historiæ 103
     - General character . . . 103
  - Characterization of Tacitus . 103
     - His carefulness in research 103
     - Nature of his authorities . 103
     - His ruling political principle 103
     - His admiration of the Republic 104
     - His reluctant recognition of the Empire 104
     - The underlying bitterness in his writings 104
     - His conscientiousness and chief excellences . . . 104
     - Lack of philosophical creed 104
     - His position in religious matters 104
     - His doubt concerning the divine government . . . 104
     - Development of Tacitus' style 105
     - Its dignity and solemnity . 105

b. — Oratory.

- The great number of rhetorically educated men 105
- Lack of freedom and opportunity of speaking 105
- Restriction of oratory 105
- Its retirement into the schools . 105

ANALYSIS. xvii

Seneca the Elder 106
  Character of his writings . . 106
  Their importance for the history of oratory 106
M. Fabius Quintilianus . . . 106
  His life and character . . . 106
  His *Institutio oratoria* . . . 106
  His preference for Cicero . . 107
  Scope of the work 107
Pliny the Younger 107
  His life and writings 107
  His letters 107
  Comparison with Cicero's letters 107
  The man as seen in his works 108
  Most interesting letters . . . 108

c. — Philosophy.

Activity in this department . . 108
Character of philosophical writers 108
Predominance of Stoicism . . 108
Punishment of Greek philosophers 108
Seneca the Younger 108
  His life and character . . . 108
  His sincerity of purpose . . 109
  Loftiness of moral view . . . 109
  Tradition concerning him . . 109
  His style 109
  Varieties of his works . . . 109
  The *Epistulæ ad Lucilium* . 110
  Seneca's views compared with Christianity 110

d. — Special Sciences.

Writers on Law:
  Masurius Sabinus 110
  Sempronius Proculus . . . 110
  The two schools of law . . . 110
Science of language 110
  Interest of the Emperors in it 110
  Claudius 110
Grammarians and Commentators:
  Q. Remmius Palæmo . . . 111
  Q. Asconius Pedianus . . . 111
  M. Valerius Probus 111
  Æmilius Asper 111
  Flavius Caper 111
  Velius Longus 111
Mathematical writers:
  Sextus Iulius Frontinus . . 111
    Life and writings 111
  Hyginus 111
  Their works on military subjects 111
Geography 112
  Pomponius Mela 112
  Pliny the Elder 112
    His life and writings . . . 112
    Scope of his work . . . 112
    His style 113
Cornelius Celsus 113
Scribonius Largus 113
Agriculture 113
Moderatus Columella 113

FIFTH PERIOD.

THE LATER EMPIRE, AFTER THE DEATH OF TRAJAN, 117 A.D.

Decline in politics and literature 114
Lack of independence 114
Artificiality of literature . . . 114
Pedantry 114
Archaistic tendency 114
Comparative unimportance of poetry 114
Literary importance of the provinces 114
Style of the provincial writers . 115

Political confusion of the third
century 115
Triumph of Christianity . . . 115
Decay of the old Roman character 115
General estimate 115

I. Poetry.

a.—Lyric.

The *Pervigilium Veneris* . . . 116
Decimus Magnus Ausonius . . 116
   His life and writings . . . 116
   Variety of his works . . . 116
   His Idyll *Mosella* 116
Aurelius Prudentius Clemens . 116

b.—Epic.

General character 117
Claudius Claudianus . . . 117
   Character of his poems . . . 117
Christian poets:
   C. Vettius Aquilius Iuvencus . 117
   Flavius Merobaudes 117
   Apollinaris Sidonius 117
   Dracontius 118
   Venantius Fortunatus . . 118

c.—Didactic.

Nemesianus 118
Festus Avienus 118
Claudius Rutilius Namatianus . 118
   His descriptive poem . . . 118
Fable 119
   Avianus 119

II. Prose.

a.—Oratory.

Cornelius Fronto 119
   His life and character . . . 119
   His reliance upon rhetoric . 119
   His archaistic preferences . . 119

L. Apuleius 119
   His life 120
   Character as a writer . . . 120
   His *Metamorphoseon* . . . 120
   Imitation of Lucian 120
   Other works of Apuleius . . 120
Q. Aurelius Symmachus . . . 120
   His orations and epistles . . 120

b.—Philosophy.

Opposition to it 121
Marcus Aurelius 121
Mystic character of philosophy . 121
Apuleius 121
Christianity opposed to philosophy 121
Effect of this opposition . . . 122
Boëtius 122
   His life and works 122
   His *de consolatione* 122

c.—History.

Activity in this department . . 122
Lack of freedom 122
Influence of rhetoric 122
Biographical treatment 122
Compendia 122
Ecclesiastical history 122
C. Suetonius Tranquillus . . . 122
   His life and writings 122
   His biographical works . . . 123
   Importance of his extant work 123
   Its anecdotical character . . 123
   Defects of the work . . . 123
Florus 123
   His writings 123
L. Ampelius 124
Granicius Licinianus 124
Marius Maximus 124
Scriptores Historiæ Augustæ . 124
   Their biographies of the Emperors 124
   Value of their writings . . . 124

ANALYSIS.

Aurelius Victor	124
His historical works	125
Works ascribed to him	125
Eutropius	125
Ammianus Marcellinus	125
His life and writings	125
The author's standpoint	126
His style	126
Defects of the work	126
Sulpicius Severus	126
Orosius	126
Magnus Aurelius Cassiodorius	126
His works	126
Iordanis	126
Gildas	126
Gregorius of Tours	126
Official state-records	126

d.—Special Sciences.

Law	127
Highest development under the Emperors	127
Civil law	127
Later codification of legal authorities	127
Most important jurists:	
Salvius Iulianus	127
Sextus Pomponius	127
Gaius	127
His introduction to legal science	127
Æmilius Papinianus	128
His *responsa* and *quæstiones*	128
	128
Domitius Ulpianus	128
Iulius Paulus	128
Herennius Modestinus	128
Collections of constitutiones:	
Codex Gregorianus	128
Codex Hermogenianus	128
Fragmenta Vaticana	128
Codex Theodosianus	128
Corpus iuris	128
Its separate parts:	
Codex Iustinianeus	128
Institutiones	129
Digesta or Pandects	129
Novellæ	129
Philology and Archæology	129
Their high standing	129
Encyclopædic character	129
1. Compilers:	
Aulus Gellius	129
His *Noctes Atticæ*	130
Importance of the work	130
Nonius Marcellus	130
Macrobius Theodosius	130
Martianus Capella	130
His writings	130
2. Writers of text-books and commentaries:	
Terentius Scaurus	131
C. Sulpicius Apollinaris	131
Helenius Acro	131
Pomponius Porphyrio	131
Plotius Sacerdos	131
Terentianus	131
Iuba	131
Marius Victorinus	131
Ælius Donatus	131
Flavius Charisius	131
Diomedes	132
Servius Honoratus	132
Priscianus	132
His grammatical works	132
Geography	132
C. Iulius Solinus	132
Æthicus Ister	132
The *itineraria*	132
Notitia and *curiosum urbis Romæ*	132
Maps	132
Astronomy	132
Firmicus Maternus (pagan)	132
Firmicus Maternus (Christian)	133

Military science 133
   Flavius Vegetius 133
      Scope of his work 133
Medicine. 133
   Marcellus Empiricus. . . . 133
   Cælius Aurelianus 133
Agriculture 133
   Gargilius Martialis 133
   Palladius Rutilius 133

e. — Patristic Literature.

The Church Fathers 134
   Minucius Felix 134
      His *Octavius* 134
   Tertullianus 134
      His character and writings . 134
   Cyprianus 134
   Arnobius 134

Lactantius Firmianus . . . 135
   Beauty of his style 135
   His acquaintance with the
      classics 135
Ambrosius 135
   His personal character . . 135
   His hymns. 135
Hieronymus 135
   His learning 135
   His translation of the Bible 135
Aurelius Augustinus 135
   His versatility 135
   His ecclesiastical impor-
      tance 135
   The *de civitate Dei* . . . 135
   The *confessiones* 136
Pope Leo I 136
Pope Gregory I 136

INTRODUCTION.

1.

IT was only at a late period that Roman literature rose to any thing like a high plane, namely, after the time when the Romans came into more active intercourse with the Greeks, and received from them abundant and varied incitement. The Roman character was in itself poorly adapted to literary development. There were wanting just those qualities which fit a people for literary and especially for poetical productions, and by which the Greeks were distinguished, — wealth and creative power of imagination, fine sense of form and instinctive appreciation of the beautiful, tendency towards the ideal, and free development of individuality. The peculiarities which make up the Roman character lie in the domain of the practical, — keen intellect, dispassionate reflection, a cast of mind masculine in its earnestness yet not youthful, inclination to work, energetic striving after the real, restraint of individuality by the interests of the whole, strict subjection of the individual to the state.

The literary activity of the Greeks appeared to the Romans as an aimless pastime and as busy idleness; even the Roman *otium* — at least in the earlier times — was filled with a more earnest activity than the free and easy *otium Græcum*, and the lively πολυπραγμοσύνη (busy curiosity) of the Athenians. On this account the Romans stood for a long time in an exclusive and contemptuous attitude towards the Greek mind; indeed, even when the higher circles had long begun to allow themselves to be penetrated by the elements of Greek culture, they displayed, in public at least, in view of the continued unpopularity of such Grecian tendencies, an aristocratic disdain and an often affected consciousness of their own superiority. With their conscientiousness in the service of the family and the community, the Romans had neither time nor inclination for purely literary occupations. For more than five centuries, therefore, nothing was produced except in such departments as from the outset made no demand for artistic perfection, as, for example, the popular farce, or such as served a definite practical purpose, as, for example, the sacred lyric, the writing of matter-of-fact chronicles, and the collection of legal formulae.

In close connection with this stands the fact that among the Romans — in distinction from most other nations — prose, which can confine itself more to essentials, was developed to classical perfection before poetry, for which beauty of form is a chief consideration.

The reason why the Heroic Epos, which forms the earliest and at the same time the brightest ornament of Greek poetry, did not make its appearance in Rome as a native production, is found in this fact, that the unimaginative Romans had no mythology rich in imposing figures and events, and that in their religion the idea outweighed the symbol.

Since, thus, literature found unfavorable soil with the Romans, a strong impulse from without was necessary in order to set Roman literature in motion; accordingly, Roman poetry in its highest forms rests in reality upon Greek foundations; and also prose, even in those departments which in their nature and origin were peculiar to the

Roman nation, particularly in oratory, has derived its artistic form from the Greeks. This permeation with Greek elements did not find its full and unhindered completion until in the sixth and seventh centuries of the city, and therefore all that was produced before this time, though often possessing originality and strength, is still crude and undeveloped, only an attempt at and beginning of artistic symmetrical production.

2.

The **Italic language**, like its sister languages, Greek and Sanskrit, is a member of the Indo-European family of languages.[1] The **Latin** is a dialect of the Italic language. By its side stand the coördinate Umbrian and Sabellian (Oscan) dialects, which, however, gradually fell into disuse.[2]

The alphabet of the Latin language was borrowed from the Greek, probably before the founding of Rome. It consisted originally of twenty-one letters, but suffered in the course of time many changes, **k**, for example, disappearing, and **g** being added. There were changes, also, in the orthography and pronunciation. **r**, for example, being often substituted for **s**, while the aspiration of the mutes first appeared in the time of Sulla, and the doubling of the consonants not before Ennius.[3]

Thus the Latin language did not obtain rules and permanency in orthography, pronunciation, and grammar until the time when literature at Rome had begun to take a loftier flight, i.e., in the sixth and seventh centuries of the city. Moreover, the acquaintance with the Greeks had a great

---

[1] Pn. 11; Wh. 192.
[2] C. 9; Mom. i. 33; Pn. 12; W. 2.
[3] C. 11; Mom. i. 281; Pn. 46; R. i. 21; W. 5.

influence upon the development of the language. Among the Romans themselves, Ennius marks an epoch in the formation of the language by introducing the hexameter. Not until the time of Cicero, however, did classical Latin take the place of archaic.

The entire character of the Latin language, as well as of the Romans in general, was peculiarly suited to prose. In earlier times, especially, the language was too stiff and angular to serve as a light and flowing dress for poetry; and in general those qualities do not prominently belong to the Latin language which are found in the Greek, and which led, of themselves, to their use in poetry. These are lightness and elegance, freedom and flexibility, natural euphony and rhythm.

The qualities which characterize the language of the Romans are, rather, an intelligence aiming at precision of expression, logical accuracy and syntactical completeness, rhetorical dignity and moderation, and an immobility amounting almost to clumsiness. Thus the Latin language was especially suited to use in prose in the practical departments of jurisprudence, legislation, oratory, and annal-writing, which has chiefly to do with the statement of facts.

Prose reached its highest development among the Romans in Cicero, but it was not until the Augustan Age that it acquired the roundness, grace, and flexibility necessary for poetry. If, therefore, we call the Ciceronian-Augustan Age the classical period of prose and poetry, from that time on a gradual decline in the language becomes noticeable. Simplicity and naturalness disappear more and more; the linguistic sense, as well as the clearness of distinction between prose and poetry becomes turbid; artificial adornment and rhetorical overloading get the upper hand; the cultivated, literary language becomes more widely separated from the language of the people; provincial elements win themselves a place. Thus arise successive periods of decline, which have been termed the Silver, Brass, and Iron Ages of the language.

3.

The following periods of Roman literature are to be distinguished:[1] —

I. — The **Pre-Historic Period**, to Livius Andronicus, 240 B.C.

II. — The **Archaic Period**, from Livius Andronicus to Cicero, 240–70 B.C.

III. — The **Golden Age**, 70 B.C.–14 A.D.
    1. The Ciceronian Period.
    2. The Augustan Period.

IV. — The **Silver Age**, 14–117 A.D.

V. — The **Period of Positive Decline** (Brass and Iron Ages), 117 A.D. to the Sixth Century.

---

[1] C. 5.

ROMAN LITERATURE.

FIRST PERIOD.

Pre-Historic, to 240 b.c.

IN the first five centuries the Romans had too little time and too little culture and freedom of movement to be able to achieve any thing important in literature. It was a time of contest and struggle; externally, for the existence of the city and state, and for winning and maintaining the supremacy over Italy; internally, for placing the constitution on a firm basis and fixing the rights of the patricians and plebeians.[1] The Roman people were in great measure cast upon their own resources; they advanced according to their own national standards and laws; not, however, as if isolation had taken place, — there was no lack of contact with the Greeks in Lower Italy; but this contact was not continuous, not sought, and not understood, and hence it lacked that deeper influence without which the Romans could not attain to a literary development. Poetry was still a thing of natural growth, without art or form, and having no ideal content. The practical ends of social life, of historical and family tradition, and of religion, gave it direction. In like manner, prose served only practical interests and needs. No genius had yet appeared to furnish rule and

---

[1] C. 23.

form to the language and literature, or give them a higher content. The language of this early period was scarcely or not at all understood in the time of Cicero and Horace; and while it has for us a high historical and linguistic interest, it has none from a literary and æsthetic point of view.

I. POETRY.

In Epic poetry the Romans have nothing which is worthy to be mentioned beside the writings of Homer among the Greeks. Neither in this nor in any subsequent period did the national spirit of the Romans produce such an Epos. Niebuhr's theory of a national Epos containing the oldest Roman legends presupposes a poetic endowment, and especially a myth-creating imagination, such as the Romans did not possess.[1]

On the other hand, a rhythmic form is not wanting, which was employed in all cases outside of the simplest notices and records. This is the **carmen** (*casmen*, from *cano*), something intermediate between prose and poetry.[2] This *carmen* employed the so-called **versus Saturnius**, which appears most frequently in the form

$$\smile \perp \smile \perp \smile \perp \smile \mid \perp \smile \perp \smile \perp \smile,$$

and which is characterized by a division into an Iambic and a Trochaic half, as well as by a certain proportion of accented syllables (the unaccented syllables can be suppressed), while, in other respects, it appears to be well-nigh without rules.[3]

This rhythm was used in the oldest **songs on historical subjects**, which — perhaps generally with musical

---

[1] C. 26; Mom. i. 291.   [2] C. 25; T. i. 79.
[3] C. 30; Mom. i. 296; W. 396.

accompaniment — were sung at table;[1] also in **hymns to the dead** (*neniæ*), sung originally, perhaps, by the relatives, later by professional mourners; in the **carmina triumphalia**, both as responsive song and with the refrain *Io triumphe!* and especially, also, in **sacred songs**, such as the *Carmen Saliare*,[2] which the Salii chanted in their festal processions in honor of Mars, and the *song of the Arval Brethren*, sung in May on the occasion of the *ambarvalia* (circuit of the fields), which, by a discovery made in Rome in 1777, has been in part rescued from oblivion.[3]

Besides the above, there were rhythmic **ritual precepts**, of which an example is seen in the *tabulæ Iguvinæ*[4] found at Iguvium in 1444. oracles, formulæ relating to the weather, incantations, and the like. Also, **epitaphs** employed the same rhythm; for example, that of L. Corn. Scipio, consul 298 B.C.:[5] —

> Cornélius Lucius | Scipió Barbátus
> Gnaivód patré prognátus | fórtis vir sapiénsque,
> Quoiús fórma virtú- | tei parísuma fúit,
> Consól censór aidílis | quei fuit apúd vos,
> Taurásiá Cisaúna | Sámnió cépit,
> Subigít omné Loucánam | ópsidésque abdoúcit.

The **Drama** appeared early in the form of a popular play, which found fruitful soil in the bantering disposition

---

[1] Cic. Tusc. i. 2; iv. 2. Hor. Od. iv. 15. 25, seqq., and elsewhere.
[2] C. 15; T. i. 81; W. 564.
[3] The beginning reads —
> Enos, Lases, juvate!
> Neve lue rue, Marmar, sins incurrere in pleores:

i.e., Nos, Lares, juvate neve luem ruem (= ruinam), Mamers, sinas incurrere in plures. C. 14; Mom. i. 294; W. 385.
[4] T. i. 83; Dict. Geog. s. *Iguvium*.
[5] C. 17; Mom. i. 579; Pn. 237; R. i. 418; T. i. 97; W. 397.

inherent in the character of the people, and in the talent for observation and improvisation peculiar to the Italians.[1] The germ of this lay already in the form of the responsive song (for example, that of the Arval Brethren); and when music, dancing, and disguises were added, the national comedy was complete, though it was, indeed, without plan, and improvised at will as a sort of carnival play.

The **Fescennini**,[2] for example (so called from the town Fescenninum,[3] in southern Etruria), possessed this simplicity, and were far from being suited to stage representation. They were exhibitions of a rather loose character at country festivals, abounding in rude personal jokes, and confined in later and more cultivated times to wedding occasions.

The **Satura**[4] also had a primitive character. This was a comic representation, accompanied with song, dance, and flute-playing, conducted at first by the country youth, but after the erection of a theatre in Rome, 364 B.C., it was placed in the hands of professional ballad-singers and actors (*histriones*). It was thus somewhat more subject to rules, and better suited to the stage, than the Fescennini.[5]

After the drama as based on rules of art came into vogue, the Satura was employed as a lively after-play (*exodium*). The same fate was also suffered by the **Atellana**,[6] a play introduced into Rome soon after 210 B.C., that is, not until the Second Period. This, in other respects similar to the Satura, was characterized by certain standing figures,[7] and

---

[1] T. i. 2.   [2] C. 28; Mom. i. 205.   [3] Cf. Hor. Epp. ii. 1, 139, seqq.
[4] Either *scil. lanx*, a dish filled with all sorts of fruits, i.e., *tuttifrutti potpourri*; or = song, masquerade of the *Saturi*, "full people."
[5] T. i. 5; C. 29.
[6] Sc. *fabula*, so called from the Campanian town Atella; also called *ludicrum Oscum*. T. i. 12; Mom. i. 297.
[7] These were Maccus, the harlequin; Bucco, the gourmand; Pappus, the bamboozled old man = pantaloon; Dossenus, the sly pickpocket = *dottore*.

was represented not by regular actors, but by masked Roman youth, and so had a higher character than the Satura.

All these representations depended, for the most part, upon improvisation and not upon written compositions, and from their lack of plan and unity, as well as from their rough and uncouth nature, had no real literary importance. Not until the following period did the Satura and Atellana receive artistic treatment.

II. PROSE.

Literary prose was not developed in Rome until in the course of the sixth century of the city. The pioneer writer in prose literature was the elder Cato. All the literary remains of the earlier period consist, with few exceptions, of short, crude records of events, laws, formulæ for worship, and the like, in which also the Saturnian verse was not unfrequently employed.[1] The conservative spirit of the Romans, the tenacity with which they held to tradition, prompted them to make official as well as private records of past events, for the most part, indeed, with a panegyric tendency and without historical conscientiousness.

Official documents of an historical nature were: a few **treaties**[2] belonging to the earliest times, — for example, that of Tarquinius Superbus with the Gabii, written upon bullock's hide, and the treaty with the Latins (493 B.C.), engraved upon a brazen pillar.[3]

Ancient in subject matter, but in respect to the time of their writing incorrectly referred to the kings, were the

---

[1] C. 35; T. i. 40.   [2] T. i. 84.

[3] The commercial treaty with Carthage, usually assigned to the year 509, is referred by Mommsen and others to the year 348.

leges regiæ,[1] old laws established by precedent, later called *ius Papirianum;* also the **commentarii regum,** which, without doubt, contained formulæ and instructions concerning the official duties of the kings.

The **commentarii magistratuum**[2] were a sort of business hand-book for those filling the secular offices, and among these the statistical tables of the censors, *tabulæ censoriæ*, were of special importance. The names of the officers were recorded in the **libri magistratuum,** of which those written on linen were called *libri lintei.*

Priestly literature was more extensive than secular. To this belonged the **libri pontificum,**[3] which contained the ritual for religious services and the axioms of priestly law; also the **commentarii pontificum,** probably a collection of legal decisions. In like manner, also, *libri* and *commentarii* of other colleges of priests are mentioned, — for example, those of the augurs.

The priests also had charge of the **fasti,**[4] which were lists of the festivals, court-days, and games, together with brief historical notices, and from which the calendar took its origin. Under the name *fasti* are included, also, lists of the consuls (*fasti consulares*), of the triumphs (*fasti triumphales*), and of the priests (*fasti sacerdotales*).

The **annales pontificum**[5] — also called *annales maximi* — were intended for public use. They were brief records of the most remarkable events, in particular of the prodigies, posted up on a white tablet in a public place. Copies of these annals afterwards formed a collection of eighty books,

---

[1] W. 253; C. 15; Clark: Early Roman Law.
[2] C. 88; T. i. 93; Mom. i. 586.
[3] C. 88, 104; Dict. Antiqq. 941; Ry. 328; T. i. 86.
[4] Dict. Antiqq. 522; Ry. 366; T. i. 87; W. 539.
[5] Mom. i. 588; C. 103; T. i. 91.

and were considered a main authority for the earliest history, though they were not so in reality, on account of their prevailingly priestly character and standpoint, and especially since the oldest annals were destroyed in the Gallic conflagration, 390 B.C. On the other hand, several **private chronicles**[1] reached back without doubt beyond this time, having probably been begun in the noble families at a very early period. Though the main purpose of these records was the glorification of some particular family, yet they were more reliable than the **laudationes funebres**,[2] or funeral orations, which were likewise written and preserved in the family archives, and contributed not a little to the corruption of Roman history.

The **leges XII tabularum**,[3] which were committed to memory in the schools as late as Cicero's time, and which were destroyed in the Gallic conflagration, were yet in existence in a restored copy in the second century, A.D. The *legis actiones*, commonly called **ius Flavianum**,[4] and published, together with the fasti, in 304 B.C., by Cn. Flavius, served as a commentary to the laws of the twelve tables. These *actiones* were originally in the exclusive possession of the Patricians.

The first and only Roman that appeared in this period as a prose writer was **Ap. Claudius Cæcus**,[5] Censor in 312, whose oration against the peace with Pyrrhus, held in the senate in 280 B.C., was extant for a long time after.

---

[1] C. 325; T. i. 94.
[2] Dict. Antiqq. 559; Ry. 426.
[3] W. 503; C. 15; Mom. i. 365; Ry. 151; T. i. 99; Hadley: Roman Law, 74.
[4] Mom. i. 598; Ry. 244; T. i. 100.
[5] C. 34; Mom. i. 580.

SECOND PERIOD.

LIVIUS ANDRONICUS TO CICERO, 240–70 B.C.

THIS period, in which Rome attained the summit of its political greatness, was, in a literary point of view, still incomplete and immature.[1] The national productions still remained clumsy and crude; the language itself needed to be shaped and moulded, but, to that end, the imitation of Greek models permitted as yet too little independence and freedom of movement, and only near the close of this period did Greek culture become so far prevalent as to gradually fit the Romans for original productions of a higher order.

The artistic literature of the Romans rests, however, entirely upon a Greek basis.[2] Greek influence, which had never been entirely wanting, became ever deeper, more general, and more potent. Intercourse with the Greeks in Lower Italy, and, after the first Punic war,[3] in Sicily, and also, after the second Punic war, in Greece and Asia Minor; the influence of Ennius in Rome after 204; the warm reception of the new culture on the part of most of the noble families, especially by the Scipios; the presence of numerous Greeks in Rome; the spread of the Greek language and

---

[1] C. 23; T. i. 103.   [2] C. 36. Mom. i. 298, 600; ii. 492. S. 5, 8.
[3] Cf. Gell. N. A. xvii. 21: —

Pœnico bello secundo musa pinnato gradu
Intulit se bellicosam in Romuli gentem feram.

the multiplication of Greek authors; the employment of Greek poets in the instruction of the youth; the increasing intercourse of the nations consequent upon the extension of the Roman empire;—all these causes naturally contributed to this result, that the unyielding nature of the Romans bent or gradually gave way before the power of the higher foreign culture. The opposition of the conservative element (like that of the elder Cato) against innovations, and the repeated banishment of Greek philosophers and orators from Rome, was no longer of any avail.[1]

This process of development brought with it, however, this result, that only the aristocracy, on the one hand, were caught and permeated by this incoming stream of culture, while, on the other hand, those literary workers who kept to the national track could no longer maintain their place on a level with the culture of the time, and lost their attractiveness for the more refined circles. Ennius, as an apostle of Greek culture, exerted a revolutionizing influence, not only on the form of literature, but also on the language itself.[2] The hexameter, which he introduced, since it fixed the quantity, compelled the giving up of the prevalent laxity and variety of the Saturnian verse and the scenic metre as to quantity, position, and the like, and aided much in forming the literary language.

In poetry the drama, and especially comedy, still occupied the foreground, but with a prevailing tendency to follow Greek models;[3] by its side stood the epos, represented especially by Ennius.

---

[1] Cf. Hor. Epp. ii. 1, 156, seq.:—
  Græcia capta ferum victorem cepit et artes
  Intulit agresti Latio.
T. i. 106; C. 91. 134; M. ii. 563.
[2] C. 71; T. i. 109, 133.   [3] T. i. 16; Mom. ii. 503.

In the field of prose we find beginnings of oratory, history, and legal writings, which are, in part, very respectable; nevertheless, in spite of the great advance made by the Romans in this period, everything still bore an archaic stamp, for which the later, classical period had little taste and understanding,[1] and which did not again find a lively appreciation until the second century, A.D.

Of the poets of this archaic period only the patriarch of poetry, Ennius, enjoyed the honor of such men as Cicero. In point of time, however, Livius Andronicus stands at the head of this period.

I. POETRY.

a.—The Drama.

Although the **National Popular Comedy** still continued, yet it was gradually giving way before the Hellenistic drama. The Satura and the Atellana were not, indeed, suppressed, but they were only attached as afterpieces (*exodia*) to the artistic drama, and, to that end, they, also, were composed according to rules of art.[2] This was done, near the close of this period (about 90 B.C.), by the poets **Novius** and **L. Pomponius**, otherwise not known to us. It lay, however, in the nature of these farces that they should preserve a popular character, calculated to excite general merriment; that they should be rude, and even, at times, obscene, as well as retain the standing figures and certain stereotyped subjects.[3]

---

[1] Cf. Hor. Epp. i. 1, 50, ff.   [2] C. 82; T. i. 5, 14.
[3] The ridicule of certain classes, such as peasants, fullers, and pimps; also, in connection with these, mythological subjects.

Far more important, however, became the **Hellenistic Drama**. At the same time, it may be noted as characteristic of Rome that, in spite of the great production of these plays, and in spite of the fact that women were admitted to the exhibitions, where the attendance was free, and so, at all events, not small, yet a permanent and conveniently-arranged theatre, such as was first built by Pompey, 56 B.C., did not exist in this period.[1] It is also worthy of note that the actor's profession remained in disrepute, and, moreover, that only freedmen and slaves appeared upon the stage.

The artistic drama, like the other varieties, still reckoned upon the taste of persons in general less cultivated, and having little appreciation for serious and deep subjects; hence comedy occupied decidedly the foreground, and especially the **fabula palliata**,[2] i.e., the comedy composed after Greek models.

This style of poetry found its prototypes in the New Attic Comedy of the third and fourth centuries, B.C., the chief representatives of which were Menander, Philemon, and Diphilos. For the most part, a love story forms the subject of these pieces, and the characters are rather stereotyped: fathers, sometimes over-strict and avaricious, sometimes indulgent and generous; young men, some light-minded and some discreet; parasites, courtesans, and finally slaves, tricky, but faithful to their love-sick young masters, and ready to serve them in all kinds of dirty work. The materials for the plays are taken from everyday life; they are not lofty in tone, and they avoid all reference to politics; hence the subject was always a general one, of wide appli-

---

[1] C. 41; Mom. ii. 500.
[2] C. 46; M. ii. 509; T. i. 19; Schlegel: Dramatic Lit. 204.

cation, easily understood, and suited to mimic representation,—all the better adapted to Rome, since the government did not favor political allusions on the stage.

Although the scene of the *palliata* was laid on Greek soil, still additions of a local character are not wanting. The technical arrangements are entirely Greek; the chorus is wanting, and the text is divided into dialogue (*diverbium*) and chants (*cantica*), with flute accompaniment. The metre is, for the most part, handled with skill, but not yet fixed in form. According to a greater or less vivacity of movement are distinguished, *fabulæ motoriæ* (especially in Plautus), *statoriæ*, and *mixtæ*.

Not unfrequently one Latin play is put together from two or more Greek ones, a proceeding which was called contamination (*contaminare*).[1]

The following are the chief representatives of the *palliata*: **Livius Andronicus**[2] (about 284–204 B.C.), who came at an early age to Rome as a prisoner of war, was set at liberty by a certain Livius (Salinator?), and became a writer of *comedies* and *tragedies*, as well as of *epic poems* (see p. 23). He was also an actor. — **Ennius** (see p. 24). — **Cn. Nævius**[3] (about 264–194), a native of Campania. He was punished at Rome with imprisonment and banishment for his plain-speaking on political matters, and died at Utica. His first piece was produced in the year 225. He was a popular, bold, and original genius, and his consciousness of his own literary importance is expressed in his epitaph composed by himself in Saturnian verse : —

---

[1] C. 53; Wr. 9.
[2] C. 37; T. i. 111; Mom. ii. 498; S. 56; Con. i. 298.
[3] C. 38; T. i. 113; Mom. ii. 519; S. 58; Con. i. 302.

Immórtalés mortáles | sí forét fas flére,
Flerént divǽ Camḗnæ | Nǽviúm poétam
Itáque postquam ést orcíno | tráditús thesaúro,
Oblíti súnt Romái | loquiér linguá latína.

Far more important, however, is **T. Maccius Plautus**, a native of Sassina in Umbria. He was of humble birth, and was forced by poverty to become a common laborer (factotum to bands of actors, and a worker in mills), and afterwards a play-writer to gain his support.[1] He died in 184.

His plays are, without exception, *palliatæ*. From about 130 which have been ascribed to him, the learned Varro selected 21 as genuine. These, with one exception, are extant.[2] They are entitled: *Amphitruo* (a parody on a mythological subject, the so-called *fabula rhinthonica*),[3] *Asinaria* (comedy of the ass), *Aulularia* (comedy of the money-pot, imitated in Molière's "l'Avare"), *Bacchides* (treating of the twin sisters Bacchis), *Captivi* (without love-plot, very moral in tone, and declared by Lessing to be the most excellent play ever put upon the stage), *Curculio* (corn-worm, name of the parasite), *Casina* (proper name), *Cistellaria* (little chest: half the play extant), *Epidicus* (proper name), *Mostellaria* (ghost comedy), *Menæchmi* (proper name, imitated by Shakspeare in the "Comedy of Errors"), *Miles Gloriosus* (the braggart soldier, imitated by A. Gryphius in the "Horribilicribrifax"), *Mercator* (merchant), *Pseudolus* (proper name), *Pœnulus* (remarkable for several Punic words), *Persa*, *Rudens* (the cable), *Stichus* (proper name: half the play extant), *Trinummus* (the treasure), *Truculentus* (the grumbler).

---

[1] Cf. Hor. Epp. ii. 1, 175.   [3] C. 40; T. i. 117.
[2] C. 44; T. i. 115.

The best plays are, perhaps, Bacchides, Captivi, Aulularia, Menæchmi, Miles Gloriosus.[1]

The following epitaph, said to have been written by himself, may serve to characterize Plautus: —

> Postquam est mortem aptus (adeptus) Plautus, comœdia luget,
> Scæna est deserta (ac) dein risus jocus ludusque
> Et numeri innumeri simul omnes collacrimarunt.

Plautus is distinguished by a popular, ever-ready wit adapted to a rude public, by genuine, telling humor, by vivacity of dialogue and skill in handling the language and metre.[2] On the other hand, the arrangement and complication of the plot is not always satisfactory. In prosody, Plautus forms an intermediate grade between the Saturnian verse and the Greek metres. In the freer treatment of the metre is seen the influence of the popular speech.[3] Plautus was ranked high in later times, especially by Cicero and Varro. He was less acceptable to Horace.[4] Single plays, particularly the Captivi, were long read in the schools, and, in the earlier times, were brought out on the stage.

P. Terentius, born at Carthage in 185, was somewhat younger than Plautus. He was brought as a slave to Rome, and there set at liberty. The fact that he was received into the society of Scipio Africanus and C. Lælius gave rise to the opinion that they were the authors of his plays.[5] He died at the early age of twenty-six (in 159), while on a journey in Greece. Of the works of Terence we have six *palliatæ*, mostly imitated from Menander, and in part com-

---

[1] Other critics add the Trinummus and Rudens.
[2] C. 47; T. i. 125, Mom. ii. 523.
[3] Wagner's Aulularia of Plautus: Introduction.
[4] Cf. Epp. ii. 1, 170, seqq.; ii. 270, seqq.
[5] C. 50; Mom. iii. 542; Wagner's Terence: Introd. 2; Parry: Introd. xx.

binations of two or more plays : *Andria* (maid of Andros), *Eunuchus* (the Eunuch, a play which brought 8000 sesterces), *Heautontimorumenos* (the self-tormentor), *Phormio*, *Hecyra* (mother-in-law), *Adelphi* (the brothers, the most successful play of all).

Terence forms, in many respects, a contrast to Plautus.[1] In Plautus we find the natural, popular tone, in Terence, the colloquial language of the cultivated circles ; in Plautus, originality and inventive faculty, in Terence, dependence and imitation ; in Plautus, sparkling wit, in Terence, reflection and study ; in Plautus, nature, in Terence, art ; in Plautus, roughness and boldness, in Terence, smoothness and moderation ; in Plautus, a vivacity often farcical, but always telling, in Terence, measured calmness.

In general, Terence is lacking in the *virtus ac vis comica*; he excels in cultivated, elegant language, dignity, artistic arrangement, and correct delineation of character.[2] For this reason he was a favorite author in the Middle Ages. He was much read and played, especially in the schools, on account of his moral tone.[3]

Amon the remaining composers of *palliatæ* were **Statius Cæcili s**,[4] an Insubrian, who came as a prisoner of war to Rome, and appears to have taken a position, in respect to time and style of composition, intermediate between Plautus and Terence : and **Luscius Lavinius** (or Lanuvinus), a rival and enemy of Terence.

---

[1] Mom. iii. 538 ; Wagner, 8 ; Parry, xvii.

[2] C. 51 ; T. i. 146 ; Parry, xxiii. On the metres and prosody of Terence, see Parry, xxvii. ; Wagner, 12 ; and on the relation of Terence to the " New Comedy," Parry, 487.

[3] The Eunuchus was translated into German as early as 1486, and all the plays in 1499.

[4] C. 48 ; T. i. 135 ; Mom. ii. 523.

Before the much-fostered palliata, the national comedy, **fabula togata**,[1] retired into the background. This had for its subject the daily life of the lower classes, especially the small gossip of the municipal towns; and since Rome and its citizens could not be brought upon the stage, the scene was customarily laid in a Latin country town.

Little has been preserved of the *togata*. Its chief authors were **Titinius**, a contemporary of Terence; **T. Quinctius Atta**, who died in 77; and especially **L. Afranius**, who wrote somewhere about the year 100.

In **Tragedy**,[2] also, the Hellenistic tendency prevailed, but the greater expense of production, as well as the public taste, which sought after fun and entertainment, caused tragedy to be less cultivated than comedy. Moreover, the Roman tragic writers did not strike the right tone, in that, with them, seriousness and pathos too often degenerated into heaviness and bombast. Their model was, for the most part, Euripides.

Beside the tragedy based upon Greek models, the Roman national play, **fabula prætexta**,[3] which dealt with historical subjects, could attain to no very important position. In the department of tragedy are to be mentioned: **Livius Andronicus**, whose plays treated of mythological subjects, taken chiefly from the legends centering about Troy; **Cn. Nævius**, who also wrote *prætextæ*; **Q. Ennius**;[4] especially, however, **M. Pacuvius**[5] and **L. Accius**,[6] (At-

---

[1] C. 55; T. i. 25; Mom. ii. 525.
[2] C. 59; T. i. 16; Mom. iii. 536; S. 129; Con. i. 294.
[3] C. 38; T. i. 19.
[4] C. 58; S. 89; T. i. 131; Con. i. 304.
[5] C. 62; T. i. 134; S. 143; Con. i. 309.
[6] C. 65; T. i. 167; Mom. iii. 537; S. 153; Con. i. 317.

tius). The former was born at Brundisium about 220 B.C., and died at Tarentum about 132. He was brought to Rome by his uncle Ennius, and was a painter as well as an author. His works consist of twelve *tragedies* and one *prætexta* entitled *Paulus* (probably referring to Æmilius Paulus). Accius lived about 170-94, and was author of about forty *tragedies* and several *prætextæ*, of which, for example, the *Decius* treats of the voluntary death of the younger P. Decius Mus, near Sentinum. Cicero, Horace, and others give Accius high rank as *gravis, ingeniosus, altus poeta*. He also wrote *Didascalica* (a history of Greek and Roman poetry), *Pragmatica* (treating of literary history), and *Annales*.

Of all these tragedies and prætextæ only fragments are extant.

b.—The Epos.

The Romans could not possess an heroic epos of their own, like the Homeric, because the needful legendary material, as well as gods and heroes, were wanting. Hence the national epic writers were obliged to confine themselves to historical subjects instead of mythological.

Livius Andronicus, indeed, the first epic writer in point of time, contented himself with a heavy *translation of the Odyssey*[1] in the Saturnian metre, which was in later times no longer readable, though, according to Horace,[2] it was used by Orbilius as a school-book.

The following epic writers turned their attention resolutely

---

[1] The first verse reads, according to Gellius, N. A. xviii. 9:—
Virúm mihi Caména | insece vérsútum.

[2] Epp. ii. 1, 69, seqq.

and with success to the history of their native land. Thus, in the first place, **Cn. Nævius,**[1] still, however, in the Saturnian metre, treated of the *First Punic War.*[2] This work, of which only fragments remain, has been well compared to the rhyme-chronicles of the Middle Ages.

Nævius was far surpassed by **Q. Ennius.**[3] The latter was born, 239, at Rudiæ in Apulia, was taken to Rome by Cato on his return from Sardinia, found there an appreciative reception in aristocratic circles favorable to Hellenic culture, especially from Scipio Africanus the Elder, and from M. Fulvius Nobilior, obtained Roman citizenship, and died 169. His chief work (besides *comedies, tragedies,* and *saturæ*) was the *Annales,* which treated, in 18 books, of the history of Rome from Æneas to his own times. In respect to metre, forms of speech, inflections, and word-formations, this work marked an era through the introduction of the hexameter in place of the Saturnian verse.[4] It is true, the hexameter of Ennius was somewhat awkward : for example,

        Cives Romani tunc facti sunt Campani,

or,

        Introducuntur legati Minturnenses ;

also in bad taste, as

        O Tite, tute, Tati, tibi tanta tyranne tulisti,

and forced, as in the well-known tmesis :

        Cere comminuit brum.

But we also find places of great poetic power and beauty ;[5]

---

[1] C. 39; Mom. ii. 540.
[2] According to Cicero, Brut. 19, 75. luculente sed minus polite.
[3] C. 68; T. i. 129; Mom. ii. 542; S. 68; Con. i. 329.
[4] C. 71; S. 91, 107.
[5] See Cic. de Div. i. 20, 40, seqq. 48, 107, seq. de Off. i. 12, 38.

for Ennius was a man of remarkable talent; he possessed a lively imagination, warm feeling, and a great faculty for moulding forms and language.[1] His work, though it was long looked upon by the Romans as their greatest national epic, put the artistic, Hellenic epos in place of the naïve national one. Ennius was particularly admired by Cicero. Quintilian says of him,[2] "Ennium sicut sacros vetustate lucos adoremus, in quibus grandia et antiqua robora jam non tantam habent speciem quantam religionem."

The *Satura*,[3] too, acquired a new meaning through Ennius, inasmuch as he gave this name to a collection of miscellaneous poems of a didactic nature, written in different metres. His successor in this department was **C. Lucilius**,[4] born about 150 at Suessa Aurunca in Campania, of equestrian family. He was a friend of the younger Scipio Africanus, and died 103. In his poems, varied, indeed, in form and contents, but without elegance and finish, Lucilius subjected, in a bold and witty manner, public affairs and personages to sharp and searching criticism; and in so doing, he gave to the Satura the character which has since been associated with the name Satire; to wit, that of an invective poem. In this respect Horace gave it its complete form.

II. PROSE.

Prose, in both oral and written form as necessity or preference dictated, was, indeed, employed in the senate and in the forum, by orators and jurists, historians and profes-

---

[1] S. 110; T. i. 133.
[2] Inst. Orat. x. 1, 88.
[3] C. 75; T. i. 32; Mom. ii. 539; S. 159.
[4] T. i. 171; Mom. iii. 551; S. 168.

sional men, but it had not been brought to any high perfection of style.[1] For this reason, the prose writers before Cicero, whose continuous succession began with Cato, and of whom our knowledge is very incomplete on account of the relatively small range of what has come down to us, were, with few exceptions, even in Cicero's time, regarded as rough, antiquated, and scarcely readable. To this archaic prose, German prose before the Reformation presents an analogy.

a.—History.

For a long time historical composition was mere annal-writing, a dry, chronological recording of the events of the year,[2] — a plane of literature which corresponds in some degree to the chronicle-writing of the Greeks before Herodotus. These annals were, for the most part, written by men active in politics, or, at least, interested in them. The older chronicles, down to the time of the Gracchi, though by no means entirely accurate, were yet, on account of their naive simplicity, more trustworthy than the later ones, which, although or because gradually more attention was paid to form and critical treatment, displayed a more conscious distortion of history in the interest of the state and of particular families and persons, and betrayed the prominence of party considerations. Some of these annals were, to all intents and purposes, autobiographies.

The earlier annalists wrote in Greek, doubtless on account of the clumsiness of the Latin language. Thus **Q. Fabius Pictor**,[3] the same that was sent to consult the Delphic oracle in 216, wrote, after the Second Punic War, a *History of*

---

[1] Mom. ii. 544; T. i. 40; C. 87.   [3] C. 89; T. i. 149.
[2] T. i. 43; Mom. ii. 550; S. 192.

Rome from Æneas to his own time, of which much use was made by later historians, especially by Livy. It is uncertain whether the Latin annals which bore his name were a separate production, or a re-shaping of his Greek work by himself or some one else. Other writers in Greek were, **L. Cincius Alimentus**, a younger contemporary of Fabius, and, somewhat later, **C. Acilius Glabrio** and **A. Postumius Albinus**.

The first to write in Latin, and the one who thus became the real founder of Latin prose literature, was **M. Porcius Cato**,[1] born at Tusculum 234. He was consul in 195, censor (hence called Censorius) 184, died 149. He was the last genuine type of the old Roman character, yet in connection with his laborious political and military activity, he was not only a copious and many-sided writer, the first prose author that could be read in later times,[2] but, also, — and nothing gives a more striking proof of the irresistibility of Greek culture, — in spite of his anti-Hellenic prejudices, he condescended in extreme old age to master Greek.

He wrote a historical work in 7 books, which he entitled *Origines* (Beginnings) because the first three books contained an account of the rise and growth of Rome under the kings, as well as of the origin of the Italian cities, probably in connection with their subjection to the Roman dominion. Book IV contained the First, Book V, the Second Punic War, Books VI and VII, the later wars down to 149.

The narrative, though enlivened by geographical and mythological notes and curiosities, was still uneven and crude, and perhaps, also, not impartial to the nobility. The

---

[1] T. i. 153; C. 91, Mom. ii. 546.   [2] Cic. Brut. 18, 69.

introduction of speeches, especially those delivered by the writer himself, was an innovation. As authorities, the old Roman legends and traditions were used; also his own experiences, and probably Italian municipal records. The work was highly valued by later writers; Cicero[1] styles Cato *gravissimus auctor*. Only a few fragments of the work are extant. — Cato also prepared a collection of witty sayings (ἀποφθέγματα); those of his own which were particularly apt and pungent were collected afterwards.

Concerning Cato as an orator, see p. 30; as an agriculturist, see p. 33.

To the earlier annalists, who, in the old, established way, treated in archaic language of tradition and history from Æneas to their own time, belonged **Cassius Hemina**, a contemporary of Cato, **L. Calpurnius Piso Frugi**, Censor 120, and **C. Sempronius Tuditanus**. The list of younger annalists began with **L. Cælius Antipater**,[2] who, about 120, wrote a *History of the Second Punic War*, with somewhat more attention to style and rhetorical form.

Among writers of *autobiographies* or *contemporary histories*, may be mentioned, **P. Rutilius Rufus**, who was consul in 105, was banished as an aristocrat, and died about 77 in Asia, — a man of the noblest character and well educated in philosophy and law; **Q. Lutatius Catulus**, who was consul in 102, and died in 87; **Sempronius Asellio**, who aimed at objective treatment, and wrote with special reference to the internal relations of the state; **L. Cornelius Sulla**, the dictator, who wrote *memoirs* from a one-sided, personal, and party standpoint; **L. Cornelius**

---

[1] Tusc. iv. 2, 3.
[2] C. 100; T. 190; Mom. iii. 562.

Sisenna[1] (119-67), who wrote a *History of the Marsian War and that of Sulla*, and who, in spite of his artificial, antiquated style, was preferred by Cicero to all earlier annalists.

On the other hand, *more comprehensive works*, reaching down to their own times, were written by contemporaries of Sulla: **Claudius Quadrigarius**, who wrote at least 23 books, beginning with the Gallic conflagration; **Valerius Antias**, who began with the earliest times, and is notorious for his exaggerations, especially in numbers, which were only gradually recognized as such by Livy, who cited him often. Hence he exerted an injurious influence upon the trustworthiness of later writers. **C. Licinius Macer** (died in 66), likewise beginning from the earliest times, wrote from a democratic standpoint, and distinguished himself by industrious use of the old records. He was much used by Livy.

b.—Oratory.

The natural talents and character of the Romans, their practical nature, their bent toward precision, pathos, and effect, were all favorable to oratory. Especially the open and free character of their political life early led to the frequent employment of oratory.[2] A certain degree of oratorical readiness was indispensable to every one that desired to make himself popular and to advance in the political career. Hence, even before the more intimate acquaintance with the Greeks, oratory was esteemed and cultivated; for a long time, it is true, without art and method, although instruction and practice in oratory went

---

[1] T. i. 213; Mom. iv. 715.   [2] T. i. 52; C. 105; S. 190.

with the Roman from youth through his entire public life.[1] Only through the influence of Greek rhetoric did Roman oratory acquire form, system, and artistic treatment, both in theory and practice.

But seldom or never could an orator unite in himself all the qualities which Cicero[2] requires,— a broad culture, especially in philosophy, knowledge of law and history, the power to change from grave to gay speech, the ability to be at one time abstract and at another concrete, and, according to necessity or pleasure, to convince and charm the hearers, and put them into any mood.

Those orators who marked epochs in the history of oratory were, according to Cicero (Brut.): **M. Porcius Cato**,[3] the first (after App. Claudius Cæcus) to commit his orations (over 150 in number) to writing. His character as an orator is set forth by such expressions as: Orator vir bonus est dicendi peritus ; Rem tene, verba sequentur ; **S. Sulpicius Galba**, consul in 144, who, under Greek influence, made use of rhetorical adornment ; **C. Gracchus**,[4] who, though not a man of thorough culture, was yet as eloquent as he was rich in thought ; the two orators, **M. Antonius**, consul in 99, and **L. Crassus**,[5] consul in 95, of whom the former was remarkable rather for natural gifts, memory, imagination, and vivacity of action ; the latter for a finer culture, legal knowledge, choice language, and wit.

The transition to the perfection of Roman oratory in Cicero is formed by **Q. Hortensius**[6] (114–50), the representative of the *genus Asiaticum*, which, in contrast to the

---

[1] Mom. ii. 553; iii. 529.
[2] Brut. 93. 322.
[3] C. 109; T. i. 154.
[4] Mom. iii. 563; C. 114; T. i. 185.
[5] C. 118; T. i. 204.
[6] C. 124; T. i. 251.

simplicity of the *genus Atticum*, was marked by a florid, and often overloaded style.

Of the works of all these orators only a few fragments are extant. We possess a hand-book of Rhetoric, in 4 books, entitled *Rhetorica ad Herennium*,[1] which was compiled for practical purposes, from Greek sources, but from an independent Roman standpoint. It was written about 80 B.C., probably by a certain **Cornificius**, at all events, not by Cicero.

c. — Special Sciences.

Among these, **Jurisprudence**[2] stands at the head, for which, as well as for oratory, the Romans were especially fitted. Roman law developed itself in a normal manner, with a national character and independence. The systematic development of criminal and especially civil law kept pace with the mainly consistent development of the Roman constitution. After the legal code had become generally known through the Ius Flavianum (see p. 13), there soon appeared a succession of learned men, who, by collecting and publishing explanations, legal opinions, judgments, rulings, and the like, founded the science of law with a success and influence all the greater from the fact that legal knowledge was absolutely necessary for the political career. Gradually there was formed a legal tradition, which was cherished in single families, as especially among the Mucii, Aelii, and Sulpicii, and which was passed down like an inheritance, as it were, from father to son.

S. Ælius Pætus,[3] consul in 198, was the author of the first law-book, under the title *Tripertita*, an interpretation of

---

[1] C. 132; T. i. 222; Mom. iii. 565.   [3] T. i. 163; Mom. ii. 555.
[2] T. i. 61, 208; C. 129.

the Laws of the Twelve Tables, later called the *ius Ælianum*, and regarded as the cradle of Roman law. Also, Cato and his son Marcus wrote legal works.

From the family of the Mucii came the celebrated jurists and authors, **P. Mucius Scævola**,[1] consul in 133, and afterwards pontifex maximus, and his still more famous son, **Q. Mucius Scævola**, consul in 95, who also became pontifex maximus, and was murdered in 82. The latter was the first to lay down a uniform and well-arranged system, and, by this means, as well as by training a large number of pupils, he exercised a great influence upon the following period.

Archæology[2] busied itself partly with linguistic matters, and partly with antiquities in general. In the former case, it had to do with fixing the written language, with etymology and the interpretation of words; in the latter, with the explanation of the antiquities referred to in the earlier literary productions. Grammatical studies received a powerful impulse from the Greek Crates of Mallos, who taught in Rome 159 B.C. Antiquarian studies, particularly those pertaining to language, gradually became the fashion, and were pursued with zeal; especially since the Latin language was brought into close connection with the Greek. The real founder of these studies in language and antiquities, and the first Roman philologist, was **L. Ælius Stilo**,[3] born at Lanuvium about 150, the most learned man of his time, teacher of Varro and Cicero. He interpreted the oldest literary remains, such as the song of the Salii, the Twelve Tables, and the early poets.

---

[1] C. 131; Mom. iii. 566–568; H. 62.
[2] T. i. 50; M. ii. 552.
[3] T. i. 200; C. 133; Mom. iii. 564.

In **Domestic Economy** and **Agriculture, Cato** wrote a complete hand-book, entitled *de re rustica*,[1] which is still extant; also a work on the same subject by the Carthaginian **Mago** was translated into Latin by order of the senate, after the conquest of Carthage.

Other sciences, such as Geography, Mathematics, and Astronomy, were not treated in a literary way in this period, although many Romans were not without a knowledge of them. It was not until the time of the Emperors that military science found systematic treatment.

---

[1] T. i. 159; C. 95.

THIRD PERIOD.

The Golden Age of Roman Literature, 70 B.C.–14 A.D.

THE most flourishing period of Roman literature is characterized and measured by the positive predominance of the Greek mind. The *amnis abundantissimus Græcarum disciplinarum et artium* [1] showed at this time its fructifying power in all directions.[2] An acquaintance with Greek works in art and science, with their home and places of nurture, especially with Athens, became more and more a necessity, or, at least, the fashion, for Romans in good society, who generally spoke and wrote Greek with ease, and were wont to pursue their studies in Athens, Rhodes, and other parts of Greece.

On the other hand, a great number of Greeks made their appearance in Rome, and were employed as teachers of rhetoric, tutors, readers, and the like. It is true they were often held in light esteem (Græculi) on account of their windy and bombastic style of talk, yet they were indispensable. For, with all the apparent prudery towards everything Greek, which was manifested even by men like Cicero, with all their boasting of the superiority of the Roman mind and nature, there yet prevailed an utter dependence in everything pertaining to artistic form. Greek writings, especially orations, were translated as exercises in the schools and elsewhere. By means of the increasing book-trade, Greek

---

[1] Cic. de Rep. ii. 19, 34.
[2] T. i. 227 et seqq.; C. 141; Mom. iv. 681; Mer. ii. 530.

authors received a quicker and more general distribution. Public libraries were founded by Asinius Pollio and Augustus. Hence arose a lively, and, indeed, irresistible impulse to literary activity. The *otium*, devoted to the Muses, gained its rightful place beside the *negotium*, in the service of the state. On a lower plane, beside this Hellenistic tendency, was the national literature, represented by only a few, as Lucretius and Varro. It was, however, by no means independent of Greece.

Within this unity of character, however, there was manifest, both in politics and in literature, a wide difference between the first and the second half of this period, between the Ciceronian and the Augustan Age, the last stage of the Republic, and the beginning of the Empire.[1] On the one hand, extreme activity in political life; on the other, a systematic quieting and suppression of the same; there, freedom even to license; here, limitation and restraint, — a shaping of thought and word with an eye to court favor; there, an almost exclusive bent toward public life; here, an accommodation to the will and taste of the court and the emperor; there, the studies which have to do with political life — oratory and political literature — prevailed; here, those departments (particularly poetry) in which the peaceful development of artistic form, that is, the æsthetic principle is prominent; there, practical results and material success were kept in view; here, perfection of form and the satisfaction of the æsthetic sense were all important. Thus each half of the Golden Age serves to supplement the other; what the one has in a greater degree appears less prominently in the other, — the excellence of the one is the lack of the other. Under the circumstances, however, it was inevitable that,

---

[1] T. i. 384.

with the empire, while taste, elegance, and perfection of form increased, independence, freshness, and energy should decrease. Literature, especially poetry, withdrew from public life, from the market-place, and from contact with the masses of the people, into the study, the salon, and to the court. Its popularity was lost in the aristocratic exclusiveness of fine culture.

In the Ciceronian Age (80–40 B.C.), oratory held the first place in importance.[1] It was then that it found its widest sphere of action, its most abundant success, and reached in Cicero its highest development. Hand in hand with it went the theoretical development, rhetoric, which was, for the most part, in the hands of the Greeks. Historical writing also flourished, but its most important representatives, Cæsar and Sallust, wrote from a political, or rather personal, standpoint.[2] Philosophy had its chief representative in Cicero, learning, in Varro. In this stormy period, poetry found few prominent representatives, — the didactic epos, Lucretius, lyric poetry, Catullus.[3] The drama passed into the mime. Cicero is to be regarded as the central point of the literary life of this period, the creator of the normal prose style.[4]

After the establishment of the Empire, political activity came to a standstill, nay, even to a state of torpor. Regard for the monarch made caution and diplomatic behavior necessary; the voice of political literature ceased to be heard; the principle of equalization and levelling, not only of the parts of the Empire, but also of minds, crippled and suppressed individual peculiarity and independence of character. Oratory and history, which flourished under the

---

[1] T. i. 229; Mer. ii. 536; Mom. iv. 723.
[2] Mom. iv. 719.   [3] T. i. 232.
[4] T. i. 235; Mom. iv. 677; Schlegel: Hist. of Lit. 77.

Republic, were now treated in a manner suited to the circumstances.[1] The former retired from the forum, partly into the Senate and the courts, and partly into the schools; the latter turned its attention chiefly to the older periods. In their place, the professions, as being politically safe and possessing practical value, took a broader field. Poetry increased in importance, being favored at court by Augustus, Mæcenas, and others, but it was confined to the narrower, educated circles.[2] It was — and, indeed, consciously and purposely — no longer popular, but courtly in tone and correct in sentiment, often more remarkable for the form than the contents. By many, poetry was written according to technical models, mechanically, and because it was the fashion. Machine poetry (*invita Minerva*) came into vogue, furthered by the public recitations introduced by Asinius Pollio.

In respect to particular departments, lyric poetry (Horace, Ovid, Tibullus, Propertius) and epic (Virgil) were prominent; also, didactic (Virgil, Ovid) and satiric (Horace); the drama remained unimportant from a literary point of view. On the whole, an extremely active production showed itself; but, in the case of the majority, on account of the lack of individual poetic impulse, originality, and inward truth, poetry was only a thing of fashion, based on ostentation.

The more distant parts of Italy, and even single provinces, became more and more possessed with this literary movement, particularly through the development of the booktrade, which was furthered especially by T. Pomponius Atticus.[3] All the famous writers of the first rank in the

---

[1] T. i. 385; Mer. iv. 503; C. 240.
[2] T. i. 387; C. 242; Schlegel: Hist. of Lit. 71; Sellar: Roman poets of the Augustan Age.   [3] T. i. 234.

Augustan Age were not native Romans, but originated from Italian country towns. Yet, at least in prose, the specific Roman *urbanitas* stood more or less positively and consciously in contrast with the provincial tone.

I. POETRY.

a.—The Drama.

The **Artistic Drama** in its different varieties — palliata, togata, prætexta — found few new writers.[1] The new plays, such as the tragedies of Asinius Pollio, Ovid, and Varius, were designed for the more limited circles, and for reading, and hence the public presentations were confined to the older plays. In Comedy, Roscius shone as an excellent actor; in Tragedy, Æsop.[2] After the time of Sulla, however, both the artistic and the popular play were more and more crowded back by the Mime and the Pantomime.

The **Mime**[3] was old Italian, nearly related to the Atellana, and mainly distinguished from it by the even greater prominence given to gesticulation.[4] The Mime was marked by caricature in the farcical action, and in the often improvised dialogue, seasoned with personal allusions; by the forced striving to excite laughter; by an obscenity carried to the very extreme, the female parts being played by women. The subjects were taken mostly from every-day life, particularly from married life, and occasionally from mythology. The play was principally in the hands of one actor, called the archimimus, and the other players (such

---

[1] Mom. iv. 689.   [2] C. 212.
[3] *mimus*, a term used to denote both the play and the actor; in Latin also called *planipes*.
[4] C. 208; T. i. 8.

as the parasite) were subordinate to him. The language was common plebeian, and the flute served as accompaniment in the song and dance.

Among the writers of Mimes were the Roman knight **Decimus Laberius** (105–43 B.C.), who was compelled by Cæsar to appear publicly on the stage as a punishment for his boldness; and his younger contemporary, the sententious **Publilius Syrus**, of Antiochia.[1] These writers introduced the Mime into literature.

In the time of the Emperors, the Mime was displaced by the **Pantomime** (Ballet), which, under Augustus, was developed into a special art by **Bathyllus and Pylades**.[2] The subject of the Pantomime was almost always mythological, and, indeed, for the most part tragical. The play itself consisted of a union of solo dancing, chorus singing, and loud orchestral music. It was the task of the dancer to supply the lack of a text by mute action. The Pantomime, therefore, demanded and produced, on the one hand, the highest gracefulness and smoothness, elasticity and litheness of movement,—in truth a "speaking dance" (diserte saltare); but, on the other hand, it led to a one-sided predominance of sensuous attractions, and, like the modern ballet, from an æsthetic and moral point of view, had a corrupting effect.

b.—The Epos.

Far richer and more fruitful was the cultivation which the Narrative and the Didactic Epos found, as well as the nearly related varieties, the Poetic Narrative, the Satire, the Poetic Epistle, and the Idyll. The Narrative Epos was further divided into the Historic, whose subjects were taken from Roman

---

[1] C. 210; T. 1. 310; Mom. iv. 692.   [2] C. 211.

history, and the Heroic, which had to do with mythological subjects, and which rested entirely upon Greek models, especially Alexandrian. Virgil's Æneid was a combination of both kinds.

The chief representatives of Didactic Poetry were Lucretius, Virgil, and Ovid; of the Satire, Varro and Horace; of the Poetic Epistle, Horace and Ovid; of the Idyll, Virgil, and, in single poems, Horace.

Prominent among the numerous epic writers are **Cicero**,[1] with his unfortunate epic poems, written for his own glorification, *de suo consulatu*, composed in the year 60 B.C., and *de temporibus meis* (concerning my misfortunes), written in 55; **P. Terentius Varro**[2] from Atax (Atacinus) in Gallia Narbonensis (82–37 B.C.), who both worked over Greek originals with skill, as, for example, the *Argonautica* of Apollonius Rhodius, and wrote a poem entitled *bellum Sequanicum*, probably in honor of Cæsar; also, *satires* and *elegies;* **L. Varius**, the well-known friend of Virgil, and writer of *epic poems in honor of Cæsar* (*de morte Cæsaris*) *and Augustus;* **Pedo Albinovanus**, author of a *Theseis*, and an *epos concerning the occurrences of his times;* **Rabirius**, author of a *poem concerning the civil war between Octavian and Antony.*

In Didactic Epos, the most prominent writer was **T. Lucretius Carus**,[3] a Roman knight, who lived 98 (95?)-55 B.C. He was the author of an unfinished didactic poem, in 6 books, entitled, *de rerum natura*. It was the object of the poet to free the mind from the burden of the fear of the gods and of death, and, in general, from the varied

---

[1] C. 184, 213; T. i. 305.   [2] C. 231; T. i. 362.
[3] C. 220; T. i. 338; S. 199; Mom. iv. 694; Munro's Lucretius; Schlegel: Hist. of Lit. 66.

forms of superstition[1] by a rational contemplation of nature.[2] The Epicurean philosophy served him as a means to this end: — the gods do not trouble themselves about men, and death puts an end to all things. The dry subject-matter and the unpoetic character of the soulless, mechanical Epicureanism, as well as the then existing poverty of the Latin language in philosophical terms, presented the greatest difficulties to the poet; still, his enthusiasm for the idea, his energetic grasp of the system, his earnest, independent cast of mind, his wrestling with subject-matter and language, and his high poetic talent, manifesting itself in the very contest with these difficulties, render the work one of the highest interest. Yet, on account of the antique coloring, and the often abstruse contents, it is not always easy to understand and enjoy. Lucretius exercised a great influence upon subsequent poets, among them Horace and Ovid. By the later writers, with a perverted admiration for antiquity, he was preferred to the poets of the Augustan Age.

In the department of Epic Poetry, however, **P. Vergilius Maro**[3] rises above all others.[4] Virgil, the son of a farmer in easy circumstances, was born at Andes, near Mantua, on the 15th of October, 70 B.C. He pursued his studies, especially rhetoric and philosophy, under Greek teachers at Cremona, Milan, and, after the year 53, in Rome. He then returned home, lost his estate twice by the distributions of land in 41 and 40, but recovered it on the petition of Asinius Pollio and Maecenas, came into intimate relations

---

[1] Artis relligionum animum nodis exsolvere pergo. i. 930 f.
[2] Naturae species ratioque. ii. 60.
[3] C. 252; T. i. 406; Mer. iv. 573; Kennedy's Virgil: Introd.; Sellar: Roman poets of the Augustan Age, 59.
[4] Vergilius was the original manner of writing; Virgilius did not come into use until the Middle Ages.

with the latter in 39, and thenceforth lived highly esteemed by Augustus, Horace, and others. He dwelt, for the most part, in Campania, in comfortable circumstances, though in poor health, and died at Brundisium, on his return journey from Athens, on the 21st of September, 19 B.C., and was buried near Naples. An ancient epitaph on him reads:—

> Mantua me genuit, Calabri rapuere, tenet nunc
> Parthenope, cecini pascua rura duces.

As a man, Virgil was an *anima candida*, gentle, pure in morals, amiable, true-hearted, bashful and awkward in appearance;[1] as a poet, especially fitted for the expression of gentle and deep emotions and tender relations, for drawing idyllic pictures, sentimentally conceived and carried out. Hence he was a sincere and enthusiastic admirer of the era of peace brought about by Augustus. Not original in flow of fancy, nor impelled by genius to write poetry, he worked slowly and laboriously with a definite object in view, patiently and incessantly polishing, and so became a model of correctness and elegance.

The probable order of his poems is as follows: in the years 41–39 (or 37?) Eclogæ II, III, V, I, IX, IV, VI, VIII, VII, X; in the years 37–30, Georgica; 29–19, Æneis.

1. *Bucolica*[2] consisting of 10 idylls, also called *Eclogæ*, a kind of poetry which is really foreign to the Roman mind, not national in its character. Virgil imitated Theocritus, but mostly with an intermingling of personal relations. Hence the shepherd characters are in the main allegorical persons.[3] The situations are taken from the circumstances

---

[1] Cf. Hor. Sat. i. 3. 2 s, seqq.
[2] C. 250; T. i. 411; M. r. iv. 575; Conington's Virgil, i. 2; Sellar: Augustan poets, 132.
[3] For example, Ecl. i. Tityrus = Virgil; Ecl. v. Daphnis = Cæsar.

of the poet,[1] and thus he writes with a definite purpose in view, — a method of treatment of which this kind of poetry, naturally naive and popular, does not admit. Nevertheless the Bucolics were greeted with great applause on the part of the Roman public, not in spite of the allegory, but on account of it, and especially on account of their elegance of language and versification.

2. The *Georgica*[2] were written at the suggestion of Mæcenas. The subject was Italian agriculture. Book I treats of farming, II, of the culture of trees, III, of cattle-raising, IV, of bee-culture.

The main object of the poet was to bring these old Roman occupations into honor again, especially in the eyes of the cultured proprietors of large estates, with no intention that the poems should be considered a hand-book for the common peasants. In some particulars, Virgil depended upon Greek models, as Hesiod, Aratus, and others; on the whole, however, the treatment is independent, because the subjects suited his individual genius and his personal experience. The tone is warm and lively, the language skilfully used, and the episodes[3] give occasion for the most pleasing variety, so that the poem "is the most perfect production of any considerable length that Roman poetry has to offer" (Teuffel).

3. The *Æneis*,[4] in 12 books, was not completed, and

---

[1] Cf., for example, Ecl. v., relating to Cæsar; i., thanks to Octavian; ix., complaint about the second loss of his estate; iv., praise of Pollio; x., to Corn. Gallus.

[2] C. 261; T. i. 413; Mer. iv. 441; Schlegel: Hist. of Lit. 72; Conington's Virgil, i. 124; Sellar, 174.

[3] Especially ii. 136-176, the praise of Italy; ii. 323-345, the praise of spring; ii. 458-540, the praise of country life; iii. 339-383, the shepherd life of the Scythians; iii. 478-566, the Noric cattle pest; iv. 315-558, the myth of Aristæus.

[4] C. 265; T. i. 415; Mer. iv. 443; Conington's Virgil, ii. 2; Sellar, 292.

hence it was Virgil's wish at his death that it be destroyed. It was published, however, by his friends Varius and Tucca, but without additions (hence the 58 incomplete verses). The poem treats of the adventures of Æneas after the destruction of Troy, his arrival in Italy, his alliances and contests with the inhabitants. The model for the first six books is the Odyssey, and for the last six, the Iliad.

Virgil's purpose is, on the one hand, to trace Rome back to the settlement of the Trojans in Italy under the special leadership of the gods, and, on the other, to show the descent of the patrician families from the Trojan colonists, especially of the Julian family, from Æneas's son Iulus. The poem was, therefore, a glorification of the Roman people and the Julian dynasty. However, the legend of Æneas had too little footing in the national consciousness, and hence Virgil was obliged to weave in a multitude of learned notes, acquired by industrious study. The least successful part of all is the character of Æneas himself, who appears not as the strong hero of antiquity, but as a weak, sentimental man, led like a puppet by the gods (*pius Æneas*).

The finest parts of the poem are those in which passion plays the chief part; before all, the episode of Dido in the fourth book. Here Virgil reaches the height of his theme. The language is carefully polished, yet — particularly when compared with that of Homer — not simple and naïve, but rhetorical, and often needlessly pathetic.

It was inevitable that the poem should win great applause with the Romans, especially with the higher circles, on account of its loyal and patriotic motive, its scene reminding them of home, and, also, from the national and local allusions, and the stateliness of the verse.

Besides the above, lesser poems have been attributed to Virgil, — Culex, Moretum (the most successful), Copa, Catalecta, Ciris;[1] it is, however, certain that Virgil did not write the Ciris. They are mostly idyllic pictures of everyday life.

Virgil was held in great honor by the Romans.[2] His poems soon came into use in the schools, and were often imitated and interpreted.[3] They were also used as oracles, the book being opened at random (*Sortes Vergilianæ*).

In the Middle Ages the person of Virgil was invested with a multitude of romantic legends. He was considered a miracle-worker and magician. Dante represents himself as led by Virgil through the infernal regions.

Among the writers of didactic poetry under Augustus may be mentioned: **Gratius Faliscus**, author of *Cynegetica* in 536 hexameters, and especially **Manilius**,[4] the personally unknown author of *Astronomica*, in 5 books, which, by their originality, in spite of the bias for astrology, testify to a many-sided culture, and are very correct in form.

c. — Satire and Epistle.

The **Satire** had received from Lucilius the character of a criticism of the existing state of things, and had taken on the form of poetry. From this form **M. Terentius Varro** (see p. 82) made a deviation, inasmuch as he united poetry and prose in his 150 books *Saturæ Menip-*

---

[1] C. 257; T. i. 420.
[2] Cf. Prop. iii. 32, 65, seq.

> Cedite Romani Scriptores, cedite Graii,
> Nescio quid maius nascitur Iliade.

[3] Commentary of Servius in the fourth Century. See p. 132.
[4] C. 313; T. i. 487.

pea.[1] In very arbitrary form,[2] and with loose connection, Varro treated of philosophical questions and the condition of his times. His standpoint was the national Roman one of the good old times, and hence opposed to modern ideas. Only fragments of his works remain. Satire received its highest development from Horace.

Q. Horatius Flaccus[3] was born at Venusia[4] on the 8th of December, 65 B.C.[5] He was the son of a freedman,[6] who, however, had him carefully educated at Rome.[7] Becoming acquainted with M. Brutus at Athens, he accepted the post of tribunus militum[8] in his service, but was unable, at Philippi, to save the fortunes of the Republic by his bravery.[9] After being deprived of his estate by the distribution of lands under Octavian, he became a scribe for the quaestors, and devoted himself to writing poetry.[10] Through his poems he became acquainted with Virgil and Varius, and through them (in 39), with Mæcenas;[11] after which time, received also into the circle of Augustus' friends, he lived in the most comfortable circumstances. In the year 37 he accompanied Mæcenas to Brundisium,[12] and received from him (in 33) a modest but finely-situated estate near Tibur, — the often-mentioned Sabinum.[13] He died on the 27th of November, 8 B.C., fifty-seven years of age. In person, Horace

---

[1] The name Satur æ Menippeæ comes from the fact that Varro imitated the cynic Menippus, who had written such satires. T. i. 238; C. 144; Mom. iv. 704.

[2] Prose and poetry, an intermixture of Greek words and sentences, variety in the metre.

[3] C. 280; T. i. 433; Mer. iv. 452; Macleane's Commentary: Introd.

[4] Sat. ii. 1, 34, seq.

[5] Epp. i. 20, 27; Od. iii. 21, 1.

[6] Sat. i. 6, 6, seqq.

[7] Sat. i. 6, 71, seqq.

[8] Sat. i. 6, 48.

[9] Od. ii. 7, 9, seqq.

[10] Epp. ii. 2, 50, seq.

[11] Sat. i. 6, 54, seqq.

[12] Sat. i. 5.

[13] Sat. ii. 6, 1, seqq.

was short and fleshy;[1] his dark hair he lost in his later years.[2]

The poems of Horace are, in part, Satires and Epistles, — both together also called Sermones, — and, in part, lyric poems, Odes and Epodes. As regards the time of publication, Sat. I was probably published in the year 34, Sat. II in 30, and, also, the Epodes, at about the same time with the latter; Odes I–III in 23, Epp. I in 20, Carmen Sæculare, 16; Od. IV was composed after 18, and Epp. II after 17. His latest production was probably Epp. II, 3, the Ars Poetica.

1. **Satires.**[3]—The contents of the *Satires* are extremely varied. A specifically invective motive is not found in all of them. In some, Horace presents to a cultivated public rather his own life-experiences and maxims of conduct, rarely, indeed, without occasional side-thrusts and stabs; thus, in Sat. I. 4, II. 1, he sets forth the nature of his satire; in Sat. I, 10, his relations to Lucilius; in II. 6, his relations to Mæcenas and the happiness of country retirement; in I, 6, the enjoyment of modest independence; in II, 2, the praise of frugal contentment. In most of the Satires, however, Horace makes a target of particular moral obliquities, or, at least, weaknesses, and ridiculous phases, either of the existing time or of mankind in general; thus, in I, 1, the constant discontent of men with their lot; in I, 2, the extremes to which the passions may extend; in I, 9, the despicable forwardness of many in their attempt to get into the higher circles; in II. 3, the exaggerations of Stoic Philosophy; in II, 5, legacy-hunting; in II. 8, the plebeian boastfulness of the rich parvenu.

---

[1] Sat. ii. 3, 309; Epp. i. 20, 24.   [2] Epp. i. 7, 26.
[3] C. 292; T. i. 439; Mer. iv. 449; Schlegel: Hist. of Lit. 74.

To such a variety of contents this may be added, that Horace, in accordance with the form of the *Sermo*, i.e., of the conversation, does not proceed in detail according to careful arrangement, but, though fully conscious of his theme, goes on with easy carelessness ; furthermore, that he does not so much attack with sharpness and moral indignation what is really immoral, as make the perversities which present a laughable side, the petty doings of men in social and literary life, the object of good-natured ridicule, yet without any lack of earnestness when occasion demands ; and finally, that he keeps himself far removed from the captious and vexatious sphere of politics. All this contributes toward awakening and preserving in the reader a good-humored state of mind and a lively interest, especially since, for the most part, such traits of human character are made prominent, as, unrestricted by national or local bounds, are found at all times and in all places.

2. **Epistles.**[1] — *The Epistles* are written from the standpoint of one who takes a settled and calm view of life ; and they are also shaped with greater care than the Satires. Beginning, at the start, with personal matters and relations (to which only the shorter Epistles are confined, as, for example, I. 4, 8, 9, 20), but generally going beyond these, Horace treats of the most varied relations of life, and especially literary life, in a style rich in apt maxims, but never over-adorned nor wanting in taste, and lays down in these letters, with a calm and comprehensive understanding of life, the results of long observation and experience. Those Epistles are of especial interest which treat of his relations with Mæcenas,[2] as well as those of the second book, in which Horace sets forth his literary views, and places as the ultimate goal, the imitation

---

[1] T. i. 448 ; C. 293 ; Mer. iv. 457.   [2] S. i. 1, 7, 19.

of Greek perfection of form in contrast to the affected return to the old Roman poets;[1] he also shows the false æsthetic theories of the times, which seem to him enough to render the poet's avocation unendurable.[2] The richest and most comprehensive Epistle is II, 3, Ep. ad Pisones, designated by Quintilian as liber de arte poetica, in which Horace, without professing to be full and systematic, discusses, with excellent and independent judgment, a series of literary questions, with special reference to the drama.[3]

3. **Odes.**[4] — In respect to time, the first three books of the *Odes* lie between the Satires and Epistles. To these was added, later, the fourth book. The lyric writings of Horace take their root in the imitation of Greek models, and especially of those Æolic melic poets, who portray in the simplest form the common human feelings and sentiments; namely, Alcæus, Sappho, and Anacreon. He rises gradually, however, with an increasing consciousness of his powers, to an independent position. In harmony with the thoughtful nature of the poet's disposition, his lyrics are essentially poetry of the reflective kind, his poems are in general the product of industry and study; for this reason lofty flights of imagination and stormy feeling are excluded, but not warmth and inwardness of sentiment.[5] Those Odes are the most successful which present in easy style the picture of an *otium* contented with itself, in agreeable, natural, and human surroundings, or which set forth in quiet tone the worldly wisdom of the poet, — Odes in which Horace expresses his own peculiar nature;[6] while those which strike a higher tone, not quite corresponding to the genius of the

---

[1] Epp. ii. 1.   [2] Epp. ii. 2.   [3] C. 295; Macleane, 696.
[4] C. 287; T. i. 442; Schlegel: Hist. of Lit. 73; Milman's Life of Horace.
[5] Cf. Od. iv. 2, 31, seq.
[6] For example, B. i. 4, 7, 22, 37; ii. 2, 3, 7, 9, 10, 14; iii. 13, 21.

poet, or at discord with it, as well as those Odes which are prompted by external motives, make a less harmonious impression.[1] Throughout all, however, we find an abundance of true and finely-expressed thoughts; and the form, first artistically wrought out by Horace according to the various metres, became, by virtue of a constantly-increasing correctness and elegance, a model for the technique of the Roman poets, which paved the way before them, and was never afterwards equalled.[2]

4. **Epodes.**[3]—The *Epodes* are related to the Odes in form, and to the Satires in subject-matter.[4] They contain, for the most part, attacks upon individual persons in a tone prevailingly sharp, and sometimes cynical.

The personality of Horace is reflected in his poetry in an uncommon degree.[5] He is preëminently endowed on the side of the understanding and reflection; his views and principles are not taken from any given system of philosophy, though he speaks of himself as an Epicurean, but they are the outflow of an eminently sound common-sense, of shrewd and sharp observation, and of a self-contained, harmonious nature. His aim is to acquire restfulness and contentment by a cheerful, but temperate enjoyment of life, by calmness in view of external things, and by an ever-advancing culture and inward deepening. In his relations with others, kindly, social, and reliable, he still preserves his independence, and, when necessary, disagrees even with

---

[1] As, for example, iii. 1–6.
[2] Quint. Inst. Orat. x. 1, 96: Lyricorum Horatius fere solus legi dignus; nam et insurgit aliquando et plenus est iucunditatis et gratiae et variis figuris et verbis felicissime audax.
[3] This name, which did not originate with Horace, denotes the union of a long with a short verse. Horace himself calls these verses iambi.
[4] C. 286; T. i. 441.   [5] T. i. 437.

the highest personages, as, for example, with Augustus, when his own views do not accord with the wishes of others. In fulness and variety of thought, wealth of practical experience, charity of judgment, kindly humor, and grace and elegance of form, Horace is a poet of never-failing interest and never-waning importance. For this reason he has always found admirers, imitators, and commentators, as scarcely any other poet has done. Indeed, the one-sided presumption of his faultlessness has led to error, as when, for example, Hofman Peerlkamp in Holland (in 1834), and others since his time have attempted summarily to cast out as not genuine the less perfect parts of his works.

From ancient times the scholia of Porphyrio (about 200 A.D.) are preserved. A collection of scholia made in the seventh century bears the name of Acro.

Virgil and **Horace**, though sustaining relations of intimate friendship, still form, in many respects, a contrast to each other. Virgil was tall, lank, sickly in appearance, stiff, and almost offensively awkward in his movements; Horace, short and thick-set, sleek and well favored, moving in society with the ease of a man of the world; Virgil, shy, slow, and stammering in his speech; Horace, ready in conversation, witty, and sharp, upon occasion; Virgil a feminine, gentle, introspective nature; Horace, cultivated by contact with the world, grasping outward circumstances with sure hold, and using them for his purposes; Virgil, a man of the heart, religious, and earnest; Horace, a man of the understanding, with a bent toward philosophic calm, undisturbed either by external things or by passion; Virgil, devoting himself from conviction to Augustus as his benefactor, and the author of universal peace; Horace, with all his devotion, still keeping at such a distance as to insure his independence; Virgil, as a poet, rhetorical and lofty, of almost feminine gentleness and tenderness; Horace, natural, clear, transparent, full of manly, self-reliant consciousness.

d.—Lyric Poetry.

Up to this time **Lyric Poetry** had occupied a subordinate position; but it rose in this period, particularly under Augustus, to a higher plane. This was true in the highest degree of the *Elegy*, a variety of the Lyric which was copied after the Alexandrian poets, but in which the Romans excelled the originals in form and subject-matter; but especially of the *erotic Elegy*, which, already introduced by Catullus, was treated with skill and success by Ovid, Tibullus, and Propertius, while Horace confined himself to the writing of Odes. Roman lyric poetry, turning away from political life, took its subject-matter from the sphere of those sentiments and emotions which are common to humanity, and which lie at the basis of song in all times.

Among the lyric poets of the Ciceronian age, the most important one [1] (excepting **C. Licinius Calvus**, of whose writings only a few verses are preserved) is **C. Valerius Catullus**, born at Verona, 87 B.C., of a wealthy family to which the peninsula of Sirmio in the Lago di Garda belonged. He lived chiefly at Rome, in the higher, light-minded circles, was with the propraetor Memmius (57–56) in Bithynia, and died about the year 53.

His *erotic poems* have reference to a woman bearing the pseudonym Lesbia, probably the sister of the notorious P. Clodius. Other poems relate, among other things, to the death of his brother, which took place in Bithynia; to his relations with both friends and enemies,—as when he

---

[1] The greatest lyric poet of Roman literature. T. i. 373.

sharply attacks Cæsar, not so much on political grounds as from personal antipathy against Cæsar's favorite, Mamurra.

Among his longer poems (not including his imitations of Alexandrian poems), the *hymn on the marriage of Manlius Torquatus* deserves special mention. Catullus achieved his greatest success, however, in his short *love-songs* and *pictures of every-day life*. He is a thoroughly naïve poet; impetuous in love and hate, he is frequently tender and ardent; full of cheerful humor, he is often cynically harsh and sharp; always characterized by skilful handling of his very varied and occasionally rare metres.[1] The common collection, arbitrarily arranged, contains 116 poems.[2]

Under Augustus lyric poetry was chiefly represented by Cornelius Gallus, Ovid, Tibullus, and Propertius.

Cornelius Gallus,[3] born at Forum Iulii, 69 B.C., was a friend of Virgil (who addressed his Tenth Eclogue to him), and for a long time, also, of Augustus; but having fallen into disfavor with the latter after his administration in Egypt, he committed suicide in the year 26. None of his poems have been preserved.[4]

P. Ovidius Naso was born March 28, 48 B.C., at Sulmo, in the country of the Peligni. He was the son of a well-to-do Roman knight, pursued rhetorical studies at Rome, filled judicial offices for a short time, then made a journey to Greece and Asia, was married three times, was suddenly banished by Augustus, in 9 A.D., to Tomi (near the modern Kostendsche), on the Black Sea, and died there in the year 17, unpardoned, in spite of the most urgent complaints and

---

[1] As, for example, the Galiiambus in the poem entitled *Attis*.
[2] C. 233; S. 337; T. i. 373; Mom. iv. 702; Ellis's Commentary: Prolegom.
[3] C. 298; T. i. 431.
[4] A romantic treatment of his career may be found in Becker's "Gallus."

entreaties. As the cause of this hard treatment, Ovid mentions[1] *carmen et error*.[2] By *carmen* is doubtless to be understood the *ars amatoria*, which may have been offensive to Augustus on account of its frivolity. On the other hand, concerning the term *error* we can only make conjectures. If Ovid, with his somewhat effeminate nature, accustomed to the sensuous and the intellectual enjoyments of Rome, displayed little composure in exile, it finds its excuse, perhaps, in the nature and position of Tomi.

Ovid's earliest poems belong to the department of erotic elegy: *Amores*, in 3 books, published 14 B.C.; *Epistulae*[3] (or *Heroides*), imaginary love-letters by women of the Heroic Age, for example, Briseis, Penelope, Phædra; *Ars amatoria*, in 3 books, published, probably, 2 B.C.; as the counterpart of this, *Remedia amoris*, one book, and the *Medicamina faciei*, only partially preserved. All the above were written in a light, and some in a frivolous tone. The 15 books *Metamorphoseon*,[4] written in epic metre, are taken from mythological sources. They deal with such myths, from the beginning of the world to the apotheosis of Cæsar, as end with a metamorphosis. The myths are freely handled after Greek models, and often loosely connected with each other. On account of his banishment, the work was not fully completed. Simpler, more practical, and more earnest are the 6 books *Fastorum*,[5] a calendar written in elegiac metre, which contains, in addition to astronomical data, a connected mythological and historical account of the origin of the

---

[1] Trist. ii. 207.   [2] C. 309; T. i. 471.
[3] C. 306; T. i. 473; Mer. iv. 462; Palmer's Ovidii Heroides. "The Loves of the Heroines is the most elevated and refined in sentiment of all elegiac compositions of the Romans." Mer. iv. 463.
[4] C. 308; T. i. 477.
[5] Mer. iv. 463; Ramsay's Ovid; Paley: Ovid's Fasti.

Roman festivals. The completion of this work, also, which had been planned to consist of 12 books corresponding to the 12 months, and which, in spite of the author's superficial methods, contains a great number of important notices respecting the old Italic religion, was rendered impossible by his banishment.

At Tomi, Ovid wrote, in elegiac metre, the *Tristia* in 5 books, — complaints respecting the troubles of the journey and of life in a strange land, together with a letter to Augustus,[1] and letters to his wife; *Epistulæ ex Ponto*, 4 books, consisting of letters to various persons whom he mentions by name; then, *Ibis*, an abusive poem against an anonymous person; finally, an incomplete didactic poem entitled *Halieutica* (132 Hexameters), treating of the fish in the Black Sea.[2]

Other poems, especially a *panegyric on Augustus*, written in the Getic language, are not preserved.

Ovid possessed a poetic nature, richly gifted and happily endowed; but as a poet, no less than as a man, he is without earnestness and self-control.[3] His talents manifest themselves, therefore, chiefly in his uncommon facility of versification, which became to him a second nature and a necessity,[4] while the labor which is necessary to supplement even the best natural gifts quickly becomes distasteful to him. Hence what he says in special reference to political activity[5] may be applied also to his poetical labor. Even the ancient

---

[1] Book ii.   [2] T. i. 479; C. 310.   [3] T. i. 469; Mer. iv. 464.
[4] Trist. iv. 10, 26: Et quod temptabam dicere versus erat.
[5] Trist. iv. 10, 37-40: —

> Nec corpus patiens nec mens fuit apta labori,
> Sollicitæque fugax ambitionis eram,
> Et petere Aoniæ suadebant tuta sorores
> Otia iudicio semper amata meo.

critics lamented the fact that he gave himself up too much to his ready skill in form, and to the wealth of his imagination,[1] and that he likes to see a stain upon what is pure and perfect in order that it may thus seem piquant.[2] In this respect he may be compared to the German poet Heine.

Living for a long time in happy circumstances, moving in the high circles of the capital, and penetrated with modern views and customs, Ovid is the poet of fine, courtly, but also of light-minded, superficial, and frivolous society. His talents serve only to entertain, without stirring deeply. He treats his subjects with pleasing playfulness, with keen wit, and not seldom with open or concealed irony, but he sinks too often into wordy jingle and trifling, because earnestness and moderation are wanting to him.

In the Middle Ages the Metamorphoses in particular was much read, and a paraphrase of it was written in German couplets, about the year 1200, by Albrecht von Halberstadt, at the suggestion of the landgrave Hermann of Thüringen.

Albius Tibullus was born, about 54 B.C., of a wealthy equestrian family, nor was he left without means after his losses by the distribution of lands in 41. He attached himself to Valerius Messala, whom he accompanied in 28 to the Aquitanian war, and died in 19.

After some practice in Alexandrian versification,[3] Tibullus reached his highest plane in the *songs* addressed to his beloved Delia,[4] and in those on the relations of Sulpicia and

---

[1] For example, Quint. Inst. Orat. x. 1, 98: Ovidii Medea,—a tragedy not extant,—videtur mihi ostendere, quantum ille vir praestare potuerit, si ingenio suo imperare quam indulgere maluisset.

[2] Sen. Controv. ii. 10, 12: Aiebat decentiorem faciem esse, in qua aliquis naevos fuisset.

[3] Cf. the panegyric on Messala, iv. 1, if this is, indeed, by him.

[4] Book i.

Cerinthus.[1] In Book II the relation to Nemesis forms the subject. Book III is not by Tibullus, but by an unknown imitator.

Tibullus is the greatest Roman elegiac poet, a truly elegiac nature, revelling in the passion of love, in the sentimental portrayal of peaceful, frugal, idealized country life, with a vein of longing and sadness,[2] simple, warm, and sympathetic, possessed of fine taste and a power of artistic shaping, as complete as it is naïve in its manifestation.[3]

The younger contemporary of Tibullus was **S. Propertius**,[4] born about 50 B.C. in Umbria, probably at Asisium. He lost a part of his property in the distribution of lands in 41, then lived in Rome, where he made himself acquainted with the Alexandrian writers, especially with Callimachus. He was introduced to Mæcenas about 26, after the appearance of his first book of poems, and died in 15.

The subject of Book I is his first, complete love for "Cynthia."[5] It was published by Propertius himself in the beginning of 26. Books II and III (or, according to Lachman, II-IV) appeared later. Book IV (or V), which contains several pieces having reference to the early history of Rome, similar to the Fasti of Ovid, was probably not issued till after the poet's death.

The *Erotic Elegy* is with Propertius the immediate outflow of his nature and his life. He is sensuous, passionate, and full of imagination.[6] The enjoyment of his poems is not unfrequently disturbed by mythological additions, which border

---

[1] iv. 2-7, while iv. 8-12 are perhaps by Sulpicia herself.
[2] Cf. especially i. 1, 3, 10; ii. 1.
[3] Horace addressed to Tibullus, Od. i. 33 and Epp. i. 4. C. 301; T. i. 460.
[4] Paley's Propertius: Preface.
[5] A mistress of his, whose real name was Hostia.
[6] C. 303; T. i. 241.

upon overloading and obscurity. They owe their smoothness and finish, however, to the study of the Alexandrian writers; and the same is true, indeed, of their forced conciseness of expression.

Quintilian says,[1] concerning the Roman elegy: Elegia Græcos provocamus, cuius mihi tersus atque elegans maxime videtur auctor Tibullus, sunt qui Propertium malint; Ovidius utroque lascivior, sicut durior Gallus.

II. PROSE.

a. — Oratory.

In contrast to the *genus Asiaticum*, — the overloaded, bombastic style of oratory, — stood the *genus Atticum*, the other extreme, associated chiefly with the name of Lysias, and characterized by artificial simplicity, homeliness, and sobriety of expression. Midway between these stood the *genus Rhodium*. The genus Asiaticum was chiefly represented by Hortensius, the genus Atticum by Cæsar, M. Brutus, Cælius Rufus, and others, — later by Asinius Pollio; the genus Rhodium, by Cicero. In the Augustan Period, political activity, and, with it, oratory, had to disappear from the public stage.[2] It retired into the Senate, into the sittings of the centumviri, but particularly into the schools and audience-rooms; while, in the place of public, practical oratory, appeared rhetoric and the oratory of the schools; in place of the orator, appeared the rhetorician.[3] Indeed, even in the time of Sulla, rhetoric had been introduced into Rome by Greek teachers, and Cicero had joined with his practice the writing of theoretical books; but the condition

---

[1] Inst. Orat. x. 1, 93.   [2] F. i. 385; C. 319; Mer. iv. 431.
[3] Cf. Tac. Dial. 14: novorum rhetorum — veterum oratorum.

of things under the Empire first brought rhetoric to its full development.[1] No regard was now paid to practical ends; the subjects were invented; the main thing was practice in form and skill in delivery. The school-orations were divided into *controversiæ, suasoriæ*, and *laudationes*, or *vituperationes*.[2]

As public orators in the first half of this period, may be mentioned (besides Hortensius, see p. 31): **Cæsar**[3] (summis oratoribus æmulus),[4] **M. Calidius, C. Memmius, C. Curio, M. Cælius Rufus;** somewhat later, **Asinius Pollio,** who represented the extreme of the Attic style, was hard and antiquated, after the model of Thucydides, and **M. Valerius Messala,** who more nearly resembled Cicero in style; in the Augustan Period, **Cassius Severus,** who, on account of the aggressiveness of his oratory, was banished about 12 A.D.

Quintilian[5] thus characterizes these orators: Vim Cæsaris, indolem Cælii, subtilitatem Calidii, diligentiam Pollionis, dignitatem Messalæ, gravitatem Bruti, acerbitatem Cassii reperiemus.

At the head of Roman oratory stood **M. Tullius Cicero.**

Survey of His Life and Writings.

B.C.	
106	Jan. 3. Cicero born at Arpinum.
90, seqq.	Instructed in oratory at Rome by Greek teachers, especially Molo; became acquainted with the orators Antony and Crassus; introduced to the study of law by Q. Mucius

---

[1] T. i. 392, 537.   [2] T. i. 544; C. 321.   [3] C. 196; T. i. 314.
[4] Tac. Ann. xiii. 3.   [5] Inst. Orat. xii. 10, 11.

B.C.		
	Scævola, Augur, and Q. Mucius Scævola, Pont. max.	
89	Cicero in the army of Cn. Pompeius Strabo; instructed in philosophy by Phædrus and Philo.	de inventione (the year uncertain).
81		His first oration: pro Quintio.
80		Oratio pro S. Roscio Amerino.
79-77	Went to Greece, Rhodes, and Asia Minor for purposes of study.	
77	Married to Terentia.	
75	Quæstor in Sicily.	
70	Engaged in the suit of the Sicilians against Verres.	Orationes Verrinæ.
69	Ædile.	
68-43		Epp. ad Atticum.
66	Prætor.	Oratio de imp. Cn. Pompei.
63	Consul; called *pater patriæ* on account of the suppression of the Catilinarian conspiracy; goes over to the party of the Optimates.	Orationes iv. in Catilinam; pro Murena.
62		Orationes pro Sulla, pro Archia.
62-43		Epp. ad Familiares.
60-54		Epp. ad Quintum fratrem.
58	Cicero, banished, goes to Thessalonica.	

THIRD PERIOD.

B.C.		
57	Sept. 4th, returns to Rome.	
55	Vacillates between the Triumviri and the Senate.	de oratore.
54–51		de republica.
53	Augur.	
52		Oratio pro Milone.
51–50	Governor in Cilicia, *imperator*.	
49	Cicero goes in June to Pompey at Dyrrhachium.	
48	In September returns to Italy; forced stay at Brundisium.	
47	September. His return to Rome is permitted by Cæsar.	
46	Divorce from Terentia; marriage with Publilia.	Oratio pro Lig., Brut., Orator, de legg., paradoxa, de part. orat.
45	Death of his daughter Tullia; divorce from Publilia.	Oratio pro Deiot., de fin., Acad. (Consol., Timæus).
44	Joins the murderers of Cæsar.	Or. Phil. xiv. (Sept. 2, 44–Apr. 22, 43), Topica, de opt. gen. or., Tusc. disp., de nat. deor., de sen., de div., de fato, de amic., de officiis.
43	Dec. 7. Murdered.	

Cicero performed an important work for oratory, partly by means of his orations, and partly by means of his theoretical writings.

1. **The Orations.** — Of Cicero, as an orator, Quintilian[1] says: Apud posteros id est consecutus, ut Cicero iam non hominis nomen, sed eloquentiæ habeatur.

Cicero was created, both physically and mentally, to be an orator. Besides a good voice, and a tall and attractive figure, he possessed an excellent memory, a power of rapid grasp and combination, fiery feeling, vivid imagination, quick and telling wit. To these natural gifts were added a boundless desire for learning and wisdom, tireless industry, and zealous and systematic study. Cicero's orations are distinguished by resistless energy, moving pathos, variety and rapid change of sentiment, fiery delivery, often by redundance of expression, by a brilliant use of those means especially which appeal to the senses and feelings of the hearer; in a less degree by moral earnestness and a regard for accuracy, in which respects Cicero is certainly inferior to Demosthenes.[2]

Of Cicero's orations, fifty-seven are preserved entire, and about twenty in a fragmentary condition. All that is known of thirty-three others is, that they were delivered. Among those preserved, the following deserve special mention:[3] *pro Quintio*, the first oration pronounced by Cicero; *pro S. Roscio Amerino*, interesting from the fact that in it an attack is made upon Chrysogonus, a favorite of Sulla; the *Verrinæ*, against C. Verres, the plundering prætor of Sicily, together with the introductory *divinatio in Cæcilium*, through which Cicero maintains his right of impeachment. These orations against Verres are also important for the understanding of Roman provincial government. Further, *de imperio Cn. Pompei*, by which Cicero secured to Pompey the supreme

---

[1] Inst. Orat. xi. 112.
[2] T. i. 265; C. 169; Mom. iv. 726; Mer. ii. 422.
[3] Long's commentary on Cicero's orations; Forsyth's Life of Cicero

command in the Third Mithradatic War; *in L. Catilinam*, delivered on the 7th and 8th of November, and the 3d and 5th of December, 63 ; *pro Murena*, a defense of the consul, Licinius Murena, de ambitu, spiced with witty sallies against the judges ; *pro Sulla*, a defense against the charge of complicity in the conspiracy of Catiline ; *pro Archia*, gaining of the right of Roman citizenship for the poet Archias : *pro Sestio*, against a charge of *vis*, together with an extended account of the affairs of the Roman parties : *pro Caelio*, interesting in its relation to the history of morals : *pro Milone*, defense of Milo, charged with the murder of P. Clodius, not finished in its present form until a later time ; *pro Ligario*, a petition to Caesar in behalf of Ligarius, an adherent of Pompey ; *pro Deiotaro*, defense of King Deiotarus of Galatia, charged with an attempt upon the life of Caesar ; the 14 *Philippica*[1] against M. Antonius, of which the most important is the second, which was, however, produced only in written form.

2. **The Rhetorical Writings.**[2] — Cicero had made himself perfectly acquainted with the theories of the schools, through the instruction he had received from Greek rhetoricians, and from the study of Greek theorists and orators, especially of Hermagoras (second century, B.C.), Aristotle, Demosthenes, and Isocrates. Nevertheless, his scientific education and his practical career caused him not to remain satisfied with existing theories, but to keep constantly in view the requirement and experiences of Roman praxis. His writings contain, therefore, a system resting, for the most part, upon his own experience. They are, in detail, as fol-

---

[1] T. i. 277 ; C. 198 ; King's commentary ; Mayor's Second Philippic : Introd.
[2] T. i. 280 ; C. 180 ; Mom. iv. 723.

lows: *de inventione*, in 2 books, a crude work of his youth; *de oratore*, in 3 books, in form a dialogue, set in the year 91, in which the two great orators, L. Crassus and M. Antonius, take the chief part. In vivacious tone and beautiful, compact language Cicero speaks, in Book I. of the proper training for an orator; in Book II. of the manner of treating the subject; in Book III. of form and delivery. *Brutus, sive de claris oratoribus*, also in dialogue form, is a condensed history of Roman oratory; *Orator ad M. Brutum* describes the ideal orator; *partitiones oratoriae* is a kind of rhetorical catechism; *Topica* is an explanation of Aristotle's Topica; *de optimo genere oratorum* treats of the Asiatic and the Attic style.

b.—Cicero and Philosophy in Rome.

The second department in which Cicero worked in a productive manner was that of Philosophy.

The first contact of the Romans with Greek philosophy was no friendly one. Ennius, it is true, translated the writings of the Greek rationalist, Euhemerus; but the very thought that danger threatened from this rationalistic movement in religion, which disintegrated and destroyed the traditional world of deities, and also the idea that philosophy,—which had, indeed, at that time, passed its culminating point in Greece, and appeared in Rome essentially as Sophism,—stood in the way of healthy, practical aims and occupations, had this result, that, so late as the year 155, the three philosophers who came to Rome as ambassadors from Athens, Carneades, the Academic, Diogenes, the Stoic, and Critolaus, the peripatetic, were, at the instigation of Cato, sent away as quickly as possible. Nevertheless, the younger generation made themselves acquainted with Greek philosophy, and it gradually became a requirement of education to have heard Greek philosophers.[1]

Of the prevailing systems, Stoicism, with its earnest morality and its practical direction, suited the Romans best, because it conceded most to positive religion, and, in general, adapted itself to Roman institutions. Beginning with the younger Scipio, the majority of statesmen and jurists were Stoics.

Q. Sextius Niger[2] **and his son** of the same name, who wrote in the Greek language in the time of Cæsar and Augustus, both followed a system made up of *Stoic and Pythagorean doctrines*. In connection with this, *Epicureanism*, and the *New Academy*, which cherished scepticism, also found adherents; the former, especially, in the poet Lucretius.[3] Others did not attach themselves to any one system, but took from each what suited them. This *Eclecticism* was specially represented by **Cicero**.

On the whole, the Romans remained entirely dependent upon the Greeks in philosophy, without producing anything original. The main point with them was, always, not the theoretical, but the practical side of philosophy; accordingly, Cicero[4] designates philosophy as *bene vivendi disciplina*.

According to the custom of the times, Cicero pursued his philosophical studies at first only as a means for rhetorical education. He did not write upon these subjects until after free political activity became impossible for him through Cæsar's supremacy. On the basis of an acquaintance with the Greek philosophers, many-sided, indeed, but

---

[1] T. i. 66, 231; C. 134; Mom. iii. 512, iv. 667; Ritter: Hist. of Ancient Phil. iv. 75; Grant's Ethics of Aristotle, i. 273.   [2] C. 334.
[3] S. 224; Mom. iv. 669; Ritter, iv. 84.   [4] Tusc. iv. 3, 5.

superficial and desultory, without capacity or need for deep and original speculations, he wrote, in a very short time, a large number of philosophical treatises, which betray, only too clearly, the haste of their preparation. In his efforts to establish a certain balance between theory and practice, he shows the greatest preference for the New Academy on account of its Sophism, that being in harmony with the aims of the advocate and orator; also for Stoicism, on account of its moral tone. On the other hand, he is no friend to Epicureanism, which was understood by the Romans as really affording license for sensual pleasures. He is only superficially acquainted with the older systems of Plato and Aristotle. Cicero's main service consists in this, that he rendered Greek philosophy accessible to the Romans, and an object of lively and general interest, in a terminology for the most part created by himself, and enriching the Latin language.[1] In imitation of Plato he throws his writings, for the most part, into dialogue form, but he is far from reaching the freshness and vivacity of his model.

The philosophical writings of Cicero are given below, in chronological order.[2] The *de republica*, in 6 books, discusses the best form of government.[3] The dialogue is conducted by the younger Africanus, Lælius, and others, and, with the exception of the Somnium Scipionis, preserved by Macrobius, and belonging to the sixth book, scarcely any thing is extant

---

[1] T. i. 263, 290; C. 174; Ritter, iv. 101, 108 et seqq.; Schlegel, Hist. of Lit. 69; Reid's Academica: Introd.

[2] Cf. de div. ii. 1; C. 178.

[3] T. i. 290; Ritter, iv. 157; Mom. iv. 728. "The *Republic* — a work to be named with all honor, and indescribably attractive, even in the fragments of it which our age has been privileged to recover — concludes with a vision of the noble-minded elder Scipio, which is radiant with faith in the divine origin of the Kosmos and the immortality of the soul." Bunsen: God in History, ii. 373.

but the first two books, and these, even, not in complete form. Most of this was discovered in 1822 by Cardinal Angelo Mai in a Vatican palimpsest. The second book contains an essay on the earliest Roman history, especially the constitutional history. The *de legibus* is not complete. From the probable number of six books, only three are extant, and those in corrupted form.[1] The work contains an outline of church and state law, based upon the principles of the Stoic philosophy. The *paradoxa* is a discussion of Stoic principles. The *consolatio* was occasioned by the death of Tullia; only fragments are extant, as is also true of the *Hortensius*, a recommendation of the study of philosophy. *De finibus bonorum et malorum*,[2] in 5 books, is a *résumé* of the doctrines concerning the highest good and evil taught by the Greek philosophers, with criticisms on the same. The *academica*,[3] in 4 books, is a survey of the theories of knowledge, with special reference to the Academics; *Tusculanæ disputationes*,[4] in 5 books, contains *res ad beate vivendum maxime necessarias*, and treats, (I) *de contemnenda morte*, (II) *de tolerando dolore*, (III) *de ægritudine lenienda*, (IV) *de reliquis animi perturbationibus*, (V) *ad beate vivendum virtutem se ipsa esse contentam;* the most interesting books are the first and the fifth. The *Timæus* is a working-over of the dialogue of Plato of the same name, — a fragment. *De natura deorum*,[5] in 3 books, is a presentation of the views concerning the Deity, and his relation to the world, especially from the standpoint

---

[1] "The *De Legibus* is fraught with all that was loftiest and best in what apprehension of a divine agency in human affairs yet lingered in the ancient Roman polity, culture, and manners." Bunsen.

[2] T. i. 295; Ritter, iv. 145; Arnold's School Classics; De Finibus Bonorum et Malorum. [3] T. i. 296.

[4] Arnold's School Classics; Tusculan Disputations.

[5] T. i. 298; Bunsen, ii. 370.

of the Epicureans (I), the Stoics (II), and the Academics (III). *De divinatione*, in 2 books, sets forth in Book I, the Stoic doctrine of soothsaying, and, in Book II, arguments against it that are often humorous. *Cato maior, sive de senectute*, is a treatise in praise of old age, put in the mouth of Cato, written in a popular vein, and especially attractive on account of its cheerful, quiet tone, as well as style. *De fato*, a fragment, was written in opposition to the Stoic doctrine of fate. *Laelius, sive de amicitia*, is a treatise in praise of true friendship, such as rests upon a moral basis, written in a vivid style, and put into the mouth of Laelius the younger. *De officiis*, in 3 books, contains a system of ethics, sketched with a free hand from the teachings of the Stoics.[1] Special attention is given in Book I to the nature of the *honestum*, in Book II, to the nature of the *utile*, and in Book III, to the question of a conflict between the two. The writings *de gloria, de virtutibus*, as well as *translations from Xenophon and Plato*, are not extant.

c. — Cicero's Letters.

The art of **letter-writing** gained literary significance through Cicero. We possess four collections of Cicero's letters:[2] *ad familiares*,[3] in 16 books; *ad Atticum*, in 16 books; *ad Quintum fratrem*, in 3 books; *ad Brutum*, in 2 books. These letters, 864 in number (including the 90 addressed to Cicero), extend from the year 68 to July 28, 43. They are not, however, evenly distributed over this period, no letter, for example, being extant from the year of

---

[1] Ritter, iv. 150; Mer. ii. 415; T. i. 302.

[2] Leighton's Critical History of Cicero's Letters.

[3] This title first came into use with the edition of Stephanus, in 1526, while the other title, *ad diversos*, is neither the original one nor good Latin.

Cicero's consulship; also, the period before the civil war is represented by a relatively smaller number than the following period. The publication, although contemplated by Cicero, was not arranged for by himself, as is shown by the publication of many letters, which set his character in an unfavorable light; but it took place soon after his death, or, at all events, under the reign of Augustus, with the special coöperation of his freedman Tiro, and his friend Atticus, who was able to give the letters value in the book-market. So much is beyond a doubt. Moreover, in ancient times, many more letters of Cicero were in circulation than we now possess.

These letters are an incomparably valuable authority for the history of that time, so much so that Nepos says of those written to Atticus:[1] Quae qui legat, non multum desideret historiam contextam illorum temporum. They are, of course, different in their nature;[2] some being of a more official character, planned for publication, at least eventually, and so more carefully considered and more reserved; some — and this is especially true of the letters to Atticus — serving only the ends of confidential communication, and therefore revealing Cicero's most personal relations and thoughts, joys and sorrows, sympathies and antipathies. Accordingly, the language is sometimes formal and carefully chosen, sometimes careless and hasty, only hinting at much, and often obscure; now earnest and measured, now lively and witty.[3]

---

[1] Nep. Att. 16.

[2] C. 183; T. i. 284; Mom. iv. 721; Watson's Select Letters of Cicero; Abeken's Life and Letters of Cicero, transl. by Merivale; Forsyth's Cicero, i. 72.

[3] " Notwithstanding the manifold attractions offered by the other works of Cicero, the man of taste, the historian, the antiquary, and the student of human nature would willingly resign them all rather than be deprived of the epistles. Whether we regard them as mere specimens of style, at one

The order of the letters in the collection *ad Atticum*, is, in the main, chronological; on the other hand, the collection *ad familiares* is arranged, for the most part, according to the persons addressed; thus, for example, Book VIII contains only letters of M. Cælius to Cicero, and Book XIV, only letters of Cicero to his family. While the collection *ad Atticum* contains only letters by Cicero himself, 90 letters from others to Cicero are included in the *ad familiares*, especially from M. Cælius, Cæsar, Pompeius, Munatius Plancus, Decimus and Marcus Brutus and Sulpicius Rufus. In the collection *ad Quintum fratrem*, I. 1, is especially important, a letter which contains a complete list of instructions concerning the official duties of a Roman governor. Respecting the genuineness of the letters *ad Brutum* (at least, those of the second book), scholars are not agreed; it is doubted by the majority.

In ancient times, Cicero's letters were much read and quoted; manuscripts, however, were first discovered by Petrarch in the fourteenth century.

Concerning Cicero as a poet, see p. 40; as a historian, see p. 72.

As regards the judgment concerning Cicero as a writer and as a man, an often depreciative hypercriticism has come in of

---

time reflecting the conversational tone of familiar every-day life in its most graceful form, at another sparkling with wit, at another claiming applause as works of art belonging to the highest class, at another couched in all the stiff courtesy of diplomatic reserve; or whether we consider the ample materials derived from the purest and most inaccessible sources, which they supply for a history of the Roman constitution during its last struggles, affording a deep insight into the personal dispositions and motives of the chief leaders, — or finally seek and find in them a complete key to the character of Cicero himself, unlocking, as they do, the most hidden secrets of his thoughts, and revealing the whole man — their value is altogether inestimable." Ramsay.

late,[1] in place of the earlier unqualified admiration. It cannot be denied that Cicero can be charged with great deficiencies and weaknesses; especially does he lack independence and firmness in political life; he allows himself to be swayed by fortunate and unfortunate circumstances; is dependent upon the moment, and capricious; even in the literary field, where his chief importance lies, he betrays a straining after effect in his orations, and haste and superficiality in his philosophical writings.

But in spite of all this, Cicero is and will remain a remarkable character in history, and Varro's verdict will have to be accepted as true: Qua maior pars vitæ atque ingenii stetit, ea iudicandum de homine est.[2]

Cicero, although living in an extremely corrupt period, was pure in his manner of life, unselfish and incorruptible; a sincere patriot, bending his efforts toward the good, the beautiful, and the true; gentle toward his own family, obliging to his friends, and especially ready to advance the interests of younger men; humane in the treatment of his slaves; a man of feeling and sentiment, possessed of extraordinary intellectual capacities, a rare gift of speech, a strong imagination, and an abundance of esprit and wit. His activity in the field of literature marks an advance in the development of universal culture. For the Roman world he was a priceless mediator of the elements of Greek culture. He raised Latin language to the highest plane of development in form; and although he was not a complete Roman character, still he furthered the interests of general culture in many directions.

---

[1] Especially through Drumann and Mommsen.
[2] Forsyth's Cicero, ii. 319; T. i. 261; Ritter, iv. 99.

d. — History.

Writers of history in this period were numerous, and, as a result of the growing acquaintance with Greek models, the perfecting of the Latin language, the increasing attention paid to rhetorical finish, and the growing interest in higher culture in general, there arose an artistic and methodical treatment of history, which, confining itself, on the one hand, to the history of the times, or to particular events, or embracing, on the other, the entire field of Roman history and even universal history, proceeded on a definite plan, and employed a method of presentation, well thought out and suited to the subject-matter. The historical writers were chiefly men who lived in the midst of political activity, or, at least, belonged to a particular party, and hence historical works represented, in some degree, the party standpoint; memoirs were also frequently written. While, in the time of the Republic, when there was freedom of speech, historians turned their attention chiefly to the present or the immediate past, the later historians saw themselves, on account of the limitations introduced by the empire, obliged to seek out more remote subjects.[1]

In the first half of this period, the writers were: **T. Pomponius Atticus**,[2] who compiled an accurate tabular view of the entire field of Roman history, entitled (liber) *Annalis*, and who wrote in a similar way concerning several aristocratic families; **M. Tullius Cicero**, who wrote a detailed account of his consulship, which has not been preserved; and **Q. Ælius Tubero**, who treated of Roman history up to his own time.

Far more important, however, are the names that follow.

---

[1] Ritter, iv. 9; T. i. 230; Mom. iv. 719.   [2] T. i. 159.

C. Iulius Cæsar, born July 12, 100 B.C., was a nephew of Marius, through whose influence he became flamen dialis in 87; in 83, he married the daughter of Cinna, and on that account was reluctantly spared by Sulla; 80-78, he was in Asia; in 78, accuser of the Optimates; in 76, with Molo in Rhodes; in 68, quæstor in Spain; in 65, ædile; in 63, pontifex maximus; in 62, prætor; in 61, governor in Further Spain; in 60, triumvir with Pompey and Crassus; in 59, consul; 58-50, proconsul in Gaul. He began, in 49, the civil war against Pompey and the government of the Optimates; 48-45, gained the supreme power by defeating Pompey at Pharsalus, and the Pompeian party in Africa and Spain; was assassinated March 15, 44.

In addition to his unusual versatility, Cæsar had also the gift of oratory in uncommon measure. As an orator, he was placed by the ancients by the side of Cicero, at least as regards talent.[1] He treated the language itself in two books entitled *de analogia*. In his youth he also wrote verse. Against Cato he wrote two *anticatones*. A work on astronomy is also ascribed to him.

Most important of all, however, are his *Commentarii de bello Gallico* and *de bello civili*.[2] The former work contains, in 7 books, the exploits of Cæsar in Gaul, from 58 to 52: Book I, the victory over the Helvetians and Ariovistus in the year 58; II, the conquest of the northern and northwestern peoples of Gaul in 57; III, the maritime war against the Veneti, and the battles with the Aquitani, Menapii, and Morini in 56; IV, the conquest of the Tencteri and Usipetes, the first passage of the Rhine, and the first expedition to Britannia in 55; V, the second expedition to Britannia, the destruction of fifteen cohorts

---

[1] T. i. 314; C. 196. [2] C. 183; T. i. 317; Mom. iv. 720.

by the Eburones in 54; VI, the restoration of peace in the north, the second crossing of the Rhine, and the annihilation of the Eburones in 53; VII, the conflicts with Vercingetorix, and the final subjugation of Gaul in 52.

There is a geographical excursus in Book IV (1-3), concerning the Suevi; in V (12-14), concerning Britannia, and in VI (11-28), concerning Gallia.

The *Commentarii de bello civili* contain: Book I, the breaking out of the war, the expulsion of Pompey from Italy, and the hostilities in Spain; II, the contests about Massilia, Caesar's appointment as Dictator, and Curio's defeat in Africa; III, the further progress of the war to the beginning of the Alexandrian War.

In these writings the lines of Caesar's character are most distinctly seen, — clearness of understanding, keenness of judgment, sureness of perception, quickness of combination, a calm mastery of things in the midst of the greatest external confusion, facility, or rather apparently an entire absence of labor, in his work; on the other hand, also, a soberness of mind, nay, even a coldness of temperament, which grasps and desires only that which is real and useful, and that specifically Roman way of looking at things, which accords to the foreigner no claim to an independent existence. In respect to style, even the ancients praised the elegance, ease, simplicity, and clearness of Caesar's Commentaries.[1] But in just this apparent objectivity lies a great art; for these works are, in reality, written from motives of personal interest, being intended to justify partly his treatment of the Gauls, and partly his appearance on the scene of action

---

[1] Cic. Brut. 75, 262: valde probandi, nudi enim sunt, recti et venusti, omni ornatu orationis velut veste detracta. Schlegel: Hist. of Lit. 70; Mer. ii. 392; Froude's Caesar, 544.

after the year 50. This purpose pervades the whole, but it may be traced more clearly in his exposition of the causes which drive him irresistibly onward, and of the motives which ever seem to him right and imperative, than in his narration of the events themselves, which (more indeed in the *bello Gallico* than in the generally less carefully written *bello civili*) is, perhaps, on the whole, in accordance with truth.

Without doubt, the Commentarii de bello Gallico were written in the years 52 and 51, and published in 51; the Commentarii de bello civili were composed, but not published, in the last year of his life.

Continuations of these works are: *de bello Gallico liber VIII*, and *bellum Alexandrinum*, both without doubt written, and indeed skilfully, by Cæsar's legate, **A. Hirtius**; also the far inferior writings concerning the *bellum Africanum* and *bellum Hispaniense* by unknown authors of little cultivation.[1]

Cornelius Nepos, born about 94 B.C., in Upper Italy, lived for the most part in Rome, without office, on friendly terms with Catullus, Cicero, and especially Atticus, and died about 30. He was the author of several works that have not been preserved: *Chronicon*, *Exempla*, *Vita Catonis* and *Ciceronis*, particularly, however, of the work *de viris illustribus*, which treated, in at least 16 books, of a great number of statesmen, generals, poets, etc., and in such a manner that Greeks, Romans, and barbarians stood in contrast with each other. Of this work, the book entitled *de excellentibus ducibus exterarum gentium* is preserved. It consists of 19 biographies of Greek generals, arranged mainly in chronological order, together with the biography of the Persian Datames, of the Carthaginians Hamilcar and Hannibal, and of Cato Maior and Atticus.[2]

---

[1] T. i. 320; C. 195.   [2] C. 198; T. i. 323; Mom. iv. 719.

Nepos followed, as it seems, the purpose, on the one hand, of extending historical knowedge among the public at large, and, on the other, of exercising a moral influence upon the same. Hence, his language is simple and popular; he manifests sincere rejoicing at the good and abhorrence of the evil; he strives to be impartial even to a Hannibal, but he falls into the error of almost always seeing an ideal character in the hero of whom he happens to be treating. In general, there is a lack of independent and comprehensive historical views; the material is often selected without judgment; instead of what is really important, often details of the nature of anecdotes are made prominent, and there appear in addition not a few obscure and erroneous statements, which testify to his haste in consulting his authorities.[1] These failings, together with the fact that the style is monotonous and impure, have led to the supposition that a certain Æmilius Probus, in the time of Theodosius, worked over the existing collection after the original of Nepos. Sufficient reasons for the acceptation of this theory are not at hand. For the same reason the question whether Nepos is adapted to use in the schools has been answered by many in the negative.

C. Sallustius Crispus was born in 86 B.C. in the Sabine town of Amiternum. In his youth he led a gay life at Rome; became quæstor about the year 59; in 52 tribune of the people; was an opponent of Cicero and Pompey, and on this account (ostensibly, however, on account of his bad life) was expelled from the senate in 50, but was restored by Cæsar, made prætor, and, in 46, sent as proconsul to Africa, where he amassed great wealth.[2] After Cæsar's assassination, he devoted himself entirely to literary pursuits, and died in 35.

---

[1] Thucydides, Xenophon, Theopompus, and others.
[2] Horti Sallustiani at Rome.

Sallust wrote three works: *Catilina, Bellum Iugurthinum*, and *Historiæ*.[1]

1. *Catilina*, or *de coniuratione Catilinæ liber*, gives an account of the conspiracy of Catiline in the years 63 and 62, in connection with which the moral corruption, especially of the nobility, is disclosed for an ulterior purpose. The services of Cicero, Sallust's former opponent, are not depreciated; also, Cato is treated without bias, and Cæsar with decided partiality.

Of special interest are the orations of Cæsar and Cato (c. 51–54) on the action of the senate concerning the punishment of the arrested conspirators, and the characterization of both men. The work was probably published in the year 42.

2. *Bellum Iugurthinum* gives an account of the war against the Numidian king Jugurtha (111–106), in which the stress falls upon the portrayal of the corrupt condition of affairs at Rome under the misrule of the oligarchy, which was exposed especially in the orations of the tribune of the people, C. Memmius (c. 31), and of C. Marius (c. 85).

At the close of the war, and over against the *terror Cimbricus*, Marius appears as the support of the Roman State.

3. *Historiæ*[2] embraces the period from 78 to 67. Only fragments remain; in particular, a few orations, which bear witness to a riper historical skill than those found in the Catilina and the Jugurtha.

Sallust is called by Martial[3] *primus Romana in historia*, and rightly so, considering that he was the first to treat historical writing as an art, with a conscious method in the choice of subject and form. His chief model was

---

[1] C. 200; T. i. 344. [2] C. 202. [3] Mar. xiv. 191.

Thucydides. Although confining himself essentially to the history of his time, Sallust yet shows a comprehensive survey of general Roman history, and a correct insight into the epochs of internal development in government, culture, and morals.[1] The existing corruption impels him to a moral pathos, which, in view of his manner of life in earlier years, some have been disposed to consider insincere and affected; but it has not been sufficiently borne in mind that a change in his moral principles and views was possible in later years.

Although personally belonging to the democratic party, or, as it might be called, the imperial party (that of Cæsar), and endeavoring to show the inherent weakness of the republican government, still, he is unpartisan and just in his judgment even of aristocratic celebrities, such as Metellus, Cato, and even Sulla, and not blind to the real character of such a demagogue as Marius. His narrative, however, is incomplete, and often inaccurate, especially in chronological matters. His main strength lies in the delineation of character and in psychological arrangement. The significance of prominent individuals in the progress of history is sharply brought out.[2]

Sallust's language is often artificially antiquated, studied, and obscure; but it is rich in thought, forcible and apt in characterization, plastic in portrayal and description, often dramatic in its vivacity and realism.[3] Some of the writings ascribed to Sallust are not genuine, as, for example, two *epistulæ ad Cæsarem, invectiva in Ciceronem*, and others.

In the Augustan Period, historians stand in the first rank among prose writers.[1] Among others, **Augustus** and

---

[1] Cf. especially Cat. 6-13; Jug. 41, seq; T. i. 348.
[2] Cf. especially Cat. 53.   [3] C. 204.   [4] T. i. 386.

his friend **M. Vipsanius Agrippa** treated of their own time ; the former in 13 books, *de vita sua*, and an *index rerum a se gestarum*, the greater part of which was discovered in a copy in the temple of Augustus at Ancyra in Galatia,—the so-called *monumentum Ancyranum;* Agrippa, in an *autobiography* and in *memoirs*.[1] Also, **M. Valerius Messala** wrote *memoirs*, perhaps in the Greek language.

Asinius Pollio[2] (75 B.C.-5 A.D.) wrote from a republican standpoint[3] a *History of the Civil Wars* beginning with the year 60 B.C. This work was not completed and has not been preserved.

By far the most prominent historian of the Augustan Period is, however, **T. Livius**,[4] born at Patavium (Padua), 59 B.C., without doubt from an illustrious family. He was trained in philosophy and rhetoric at Rome ; soon took up his permanent residence there, where he came into intimate relations with Augustus ; remained without office or political activity, and died 17 A.D. in his native city, where a mausoleum was raised to him in 1548.

Besides rhetorical and philosophical writings (*dialogi*), which have not come down to us, he wrote a history of Rome, from Æneas to at least 9 B.C., in 142 books,[5] entitled *ab urbe condita libri*. Of these have been preserved Books I-X and XXI-XLV, which embrace the period 754-293 and 218-167. The loss of the other books is poorly supplied by the *periochæ* or *epitomæ*.

Livy's purpose was,[6] in contrast to the unsatisfying and degenerate present, to call to life again the better past, which

---

[1] T. i. 393. [2] T. i. 398. [3] Cf. Hor. Od. ii. 1.
[4] T. i. 492; C. 322; Mer. iv. 436; Seeley's Livy: Introd.
[5] Probably designed to reach the number of 150, to the death of Augustus.
[6] Cf. præfatio.

appeared to him in an ideal light, and, in his history, to hold before his contemporaries a picture of morality.[1]

For this Livy possessed the necessary qualities, — some of them, indeed, in rich measure, — a vivid imagination, moral sensitiveness, a warm heart, love of the truth, a genuine sympathy for the good and noble, and a natural oratorical power, cultivated in the schools of rhetoric.

The ancients gave prominence to the following qualities as belonging to him: Mira facundia, jucunditas, candor, lactea ubertas.[2] Livius candidissimus omnium magnorum ingeniorum æstimator.[3] In religious matters he holds fast to the traditional and positive as the foundation of the Roman state. He attaches value to prodigies and ceremonies, although he sometimes gives utterance to fatalistic views. In political matters he is an admirer of the Republic and of the rule of the Optimates,[4] yet probably without any deep, settled conviction, and, at all events, without any dangerous inclination to oppose the Empire. The weakest side of his work is his account of the internal development of the Roman State.[5] Concerning the earlier Roman government, especially the true relation of things during the conflict between Patricians and Plebeians, and also concerning military affairs, he has often incorrect, and even radically false, views; also, he does not trouble himself carefully to study the existing records and monuments; he brings, rather, the externals of history, especially wars, into the foreground.

---

[1] See, especially, præf. § 10: the present offers no hope, and cannot be improved, — nec vitia nostra nec remedia pati possumus; history presents enough examples both of those things which should be done, and of those which should be left undone.

[2] Quint. Inst. Orat. xi. 101.   [3] Sen. Suas. vi. 21, seq.

[4] Hence called by Augustus, Pompeianus, Tac. Ann. iv. 34.

[5] C. 327.

Among the Roman annalists he makes special use of the later ones; among others, of Licinius Macer and Valerius Antias, whose untrustworthiness he discovers only in the progress of his work. He employs them often without discrimination, consistency, or independent judgment. From the third decade on, he makes use, for the most part, of Polybius, but without the requisite care; on which account, mistakes, repetitions, and contradictions not unfrequently occur. The arrangement of events is, in the main, the traditional annalistic one.[1]

These failings, however, are gladly forgotten in view of his love for the truth, only now and then repressed by patriotism and tradition, — as, for example, in his treatment of Hannibal; — in view of his generous, humane temper of mind, the grace, clearness, and ease of his presentation,[2] the charming poetic coloring with which he invests particularly the oldest history, and the brilliant rhetoric which he displays in the numerous speeches.[3]

Livy's talents found, even in his lifetime, great recognition,[4] though Asinius Pollio thought he discovered a certain provincial tone (Patavinitas), the nature of which is, for us, at least, difficult to discover.

As early as 500 A.D., the work was divided into decades, of which the third, containing the Second Punic War, — the finest part of the work, — was most frequently read and copied.[5]

---

[1] C. 325.

[2] Quintilian compares him, in this respect, to Herodotus.

[3] T. i. 497; C. 329; Mer. iv. 438; Schlegel: Hist. of Lit. 74.

[4] According to Pliny, Epp. ii. 3, a man made a journey from Gades to Rome for the express purpose of seeing Livy.

[5] In the seventeenth century, the philologist, J. Freinsheim, born at Ulm, and Professor at Upsala and Heidelberg, attempted to supply the missing books in Livy's style.

Pompeius Trogus, a contemporary of Livy, wrote *historiæ philippicæ* in 44 books, a universal history from Ninus down to his own time, in which special regard was paid to Macedonia and the period of Alexander's successors, while Roman history was treated with comparative neglect. The work is extant only in the brief, dry compendium made by **Iustinus**, probably about the year 150 A.D. The epitome, which professedly "omitted what was neither entertaining nor necessary," was prepared with little judgment.

The **acta senatus**[1] and the **acta populi**[2] (Romani) constituted an historical authority. The former were protocols of the senate, which, according to a regulation of Cæsar, were, after the year 59, recorded and published, but which, afterwards, according to an edict of Augustus, were only recorded; the latter,[3] a daily record which contained all sorts of official and private news, and was kept up through the entire period of the emperors, but of which no genuine remains are preserved. Both of these *acta* were placed for safe keeping in the Tabularium, and could there be consulted for literary purposes.

e.—Special Sciences.

M. Terentius Varro[4] was active partly in the department of history, and partly in different fields of special science. He was born in 116 B.C. at Reate in Sabinum; was a follower of Pompey, for whom he fought unsuccessfully in Spain in the year 49; was pardoned by Cæsar, and appointed superintendent of the public library; was proscribed in 43, but made his escape, and died in the year 27. He was the most learned man and the most prolific

---

[1] Also called *publica*, or *diurna*.
[2] T. i. 379; Mom. iv. 722.
[3] Mer. iv. 330.
[4] T. i. 236; C. 142.

author of ancient Rome, a polyhistor in the highest sense. His knowledge and his writings embraced almost all conceivable subjects. The entire number of his writings amounted to over 70 works, in more than 600 volumes. Among his poetical productions, the *Saturæ Menippeæ* (see p. 45) are worthy of special mention. Of his prose works,[1] the most important are: *Libri IX disciplinarum*, an encyclopædia of the sciences, especially of the later so-called seven liberal arts, the *trivium* (*grammar, dialectics,* and *rhetoric*), and the *quadrivium* (*arithmetic, geometry, astronomy,* and *music*), and, besides these, *medicine* and *architecture*; the *imagines,* or *hebdomades,* in 15 books, containing portraits of celebrated Greeks and Romans, with short metrical explanations. Roman antiquities were treated in the *libri XLI antiquitatum,* of which *res humanæ* embraced 25 books, and *res divinæ* 16; and in a series of monographs, as, for example, *de gente populi Romani, de vita populi Romani, ætia* (= αἴτια), explanations of Roman customs, etc. The history of literature was represented by numerous writings having special reference to the technique of the drama; law, by *libri X de jure civili;* philology, by *libri XXV de lingua Latina,*[2] of which Books V-X are preserved, though incomplete and corrupt,—a collection of material which he had not worked over into proper shape; agriculture, by *libri III rerum rusticarum,* almost entirely preserved, and treating of tillage, cattle-raising, poultry-breeding, and fish-culture.

In all these works the subject-matter possesses for Varro the chief interest, while little value is attached to the form. Hence the language is uneven and frequently mixed with plebeian and archaic elements. Not unfrequently, however,

---

[1] T. i. 241; C. 146.   [2] T. i. 247; C. 151; Mom. iv. 730.

a quaint humor appears. His standpoint is specifically Roman, yet he does not ignore Greek culture. On account of the abundant material which his works contained, Varro was much used by later writers, especially by Augustine, and thus many separate passages have been preserved.

Other writers on special sciences follow. In **Law, S. Sulpicius Rufus**[1] and **A. Ofilius** were important. The former was born 105 B.C., was consul in 51, and died in 43; he was a friend of Cicero, and the most learned jurist of his time, and also the author of numerous works; Ofilius, his pupil, was also a very prolific writer, and held in high esteem, especially by Cæsar. **C. Trebatius Testa**, born about 90, was a high legal authority in Augustus' time. His pupil was **M. Antistius Labeo**[2] (60 B.C.–11 A.D.), who, in respect to thorough and comprehensive learning, as well as independence of character and political attitude, stood far above his rival, **C. Ateius Capito** (34 B.C.–21 A.D.), who courted the favor of Augustus, and was preferred by him. Both were copious writers.

Archæology and **Philology** were represented (besides by Varro) by **P. Nigidius Figulus**[3] (d. 45 B.C.), who wrote *commentarii grammatici*, in 30 books, as well as works on *theology* and *natural science;* also by **M. Verrius Flaccus**,[4] a freedman, whom Augustus chose as teacher for his grand-children, and who died under Tiberius. He wrote *fasti*, and a very learned antiquarian work, *de verborum significatu*, of which, probably in the middle of the second century, A.D., **Pompeius Festus** made an epitome, which has been in part preserved, from which, in turn, a priest named Paulus, living under Charlemagne, made excerpts. In spite of the corrupt form in which the epitomists have left this

---

[1] T. i. 257; C. 157.
[2] T. i. 387, 526.
[3] T. i. 327; C. 158; Mom. iv. 669.
[4] T. i. 511; C. 333.

work, the extant portions are of value as a repository of facts. **Iulius Hyginus,**[1] a freedman of Augustus, and director of the Palatine Library, wrote numerous works on *geography, history, agriculture,* etc.; also *commentaries on Virgil.* His 277 *Fables,* a hand-book of Mythology, the present form of which does not, however, go back to Hyginus, and 4 books *de astronomia,* are, in great part, preserved.

In **Architecture,** we possess 10 Books *de architectura,* by the architect **Vitruvius Pollio.**[2] Books I-VII treat of buildings, VIII, of aqueducts, IX, of instruments for measuring time, X, of machines. The work is dedicated to Augustus, and is rich and comprehensive in its contents, but is written in an uneven and often awkward style.

For **Geography,** — besides the already-mentioned writings of Varro and Hyginus, and exclusive of notes of travel, and occasional remarks in historical and other works, — the survey of the Roman Empire was important, which was set on foot by Cæsar, and completed under Augustus in 19 B.C. In this undertaking **Agrippa**[3] took an active part, by drawing up lists of mountains, bodies of water, and boundaries of places, and also by sketching a map of the world; for which reason, after his death, a tablet representing the world, and based upon this sketch, was placed by Augustus in the colonnade which bore Agrippa's name.

---

[1] T. i 515.   [2] T. i. 522; C. 331.   [3] T. i. 217; Mer. iv. 323.

FOURTH PERIOD.

THE SILVER AGE OF ROMAN LITERATURE, 14–117 A.D., FROM TIBERIUS TO THE DEATH OF TRAJAN.

THE Ciceronian and Augustan Periods left to the following generations an unusually rich literary inheritance, but the rule of the imperial despots from Tiberius to Domitian (interrupted only by the brief reigns of Vespasian and Titus, 70–81), that is, almost the whole of the first century after Christ, was extremely unfavorable for increasing this inheritance, or for making it profitable and fruitful. The persistent suppression of freedom in thought, word, and deed; the closing up of those avenues of activity in which the Roman mind had shown an original and creative power, namely, oratory and history; the complete cessation of political life, resulted either in resignation and apathy, or in stifled animosity and secret opposition, or in servile fawning and flattery.[1] Prevented from speaking in a simple, natural, and straightforward manner, the writers of this period sought to supply the want, of which they were only too deeply conscious, by a pathos incommensurate with the subject, by a pretentious, but often empty, play with figures of speech and sententious phrases, by a sort of significant obscurity and conciseness, and by a forced striving after contrast and striking effects. Just as in life, so in speaking and writing, there was a lack of naturalness and frankness;

---

[1] T. ii. 2, C. 311; Mer. v. 261; Schlegel: Hist. of Lit. 75.

men were conscious of being watched everywhere and at all times, and thus were obliged to be watchful in return; since their true thoughts and feelings had to shun the light of day, they fell into a habit of playing a part, into a false artificiality, into a disgusted aversion to what was near and healthy, into affectation and mannerism, and in these deviations and wanderings which were, in themselves, a clear sign of retrogression and approaching downfall, they became wont to see even an excellence and an advance; they came to delight in this state of things, and, consciously or unconsciously, helped to make it worse. For the same reason, the language of the so-called Silver Age took on a very different character from that of the Ciceronian, or even of the Augustan Period.[1] The vocabulary became much changed, partly by the invention of new words and phrases, and still more by the loss and rejection of those which had hitherto been in use; rhetorical figures took the place of the proper and natural expression; the rounded periods of a Cicero or a Livy were broken up into short, detached sentences, often having scarcely any connection with each other; the law of objectivity, the universal law of language, was destroyed by subjectivity and arbitrariness; prose and poetry were massed together without preserving definite lines of demarcation, and without a fine sense of the difference between them. The type of this style is Seneca; Quintilian in vain attempted an opposition to it.

Although, in spite of all unfavorable circumstances, there were still influences which were favorable to literature, — knowledge and use of the literary treasures of earlier times, the increase of the book-trade, the ever more frequent founding and using of libraries, the frequenting of public readings

---

[1] T. ii. 4.

(*recitationes*), — nevertheless, all this was of service to literature only so far as the latter was inoffensive and without danger to the government. Hence poetry and rhetoric stood in the foreground; both were universally employed in the education of youth, and hence universally practiced.[1] Poetry, however, was followed, in the main, from no inward impulse, was without originality and inner truth; it acquired a learned character, for which reason the poets of this period were often called *docti;* hence the unreal and manufactured lyric poetry of this period is worthless.

Epic poetry is most abundantly represented, especially because this could draw rich and exhaustless material from the safe realm of mythology. The Greek and Roman poets of the Augustan Period, particularly Virgil and Ovid, were imitated and reproduced; such poetry won praise and money (*honos et præmium*), since even the majority of the emperors had a taste for it. Domitian himself introduced a poetical contest with the conferring of a poet's wreath upon the victor. On the whole, however, it was only an artificial, labored, amateur poetry, or a restrained, calculating, servile poetry.

Oratory, in the lack of a public theatre of action, confined itself to the exercises of the schools, taking the form of *declamationes, suasoriæ,* especially *controversiæ,*[2] in which, by preference, such questions were discussed as lay far from reality, nay even from probability and possibility.

Learning, especially as represented by the elder Pliny, took an important position beside oratory.

History, during the period of depotism, was obliged either to be altogether silent, or, when it did not flatter, to be cultivated in secret. A greater freedom of movement, which

---

[1] T. ii. 7.   [2] T. i. 544; C. 321.

made a new impulse possible for historical writing as well as for satire, began first under Nerva and Trajan.

Rome remained, it is true, in this, as in former periods, the central point, controlling literary culture and production; yet literary names appear more and more not from Italy alone, but also from many provinces, especially Spain and Gaul.

I. POETRY.

a.—The Drama.

On the stage the **Mime** and the **Pantomime**[1] (see p. 38), in this, as in the foregoing period, retained a decided predominance. Whatever else was produced in the drama, especially in tragedy, was mostly designed, not for representation, but for private reading and recitation. As tragic poets are mentioned: **Pomponius Secundus**,[2] who lived under Tiberius and Caligula, and was reckoned by Quintilian as the foremost tragic writer of his time; somewhat later, **Curiatius Maternus**[3] (the same that appears in the *Dialogus* of Tacitus), who composed *mythological tragedies* and *praetextae* of a liberal tendency, as, for example, the *Cato*.

From this period are extant only the 10 *tragedies*[4] of the philosopher **Seneca**, of which 8 are complete and 2 incomplete. They all take their subjects from Greek mythology, and are composed according to Greek models, but are so rhetorical in their composition that their dramatic character is thereby lost. Seneca's authorship of these ten plays is not to be doubted; on the other hand the praetexta *Octavia*, also ascribed to him, wherein the fate of the unfortunate wife of

---

[1] T. i. 8.
[2] T. ii. 32; C. 350.
[3] T. ii. 116; Mer. vii. 30.
[4] T. ii. 49; C. 374.

Nero is treated, certainly did not originate with Seneca. On account of the correctness of the versification and the abundance of maxims, these tragedies served as models for the French tragic writers, Corneille, Racine, and others. An unfinished tragedy of **Lucan** is mentioned.

b.—The Epos.

This was partly historical and partly mythological. A poem by the emperor **Nero**, entitled *Troica*,[1] is cited, from which, probably, the ἅλωσις Ἰλίου was taken, which Nero sung with the accompaniment of the cithara, at the burning of Rome in the year 64 A.D.

The most important epic poet of this period was **M. Annæus Lucanus**,[2] born 39 A.D., at Corduba in Spain. He was the nephew of the philosopher Seneca; was educated at Rome, and, for a long time, the favorite and panegyrist of Nero; afterwards, however, he fell into disfavor, ostensibly because Nero was jealous of Lucan's fame as a poet.[3] For that reason, he took part in the conspiracy of Piso, and, after the discovery of the same, was compelled, in the year 65, to commit suicide by opening his veins. Of his poems of various kinds,[4] there remains only the *Pharsalia*[5] (incomplete), in 10 books, which treats of the civil war between Cæsar and Pompey to the time of Cæsar's blockade at Alexandria, written in a very, one might say, too historical manner,[6] and with a positive and designedly one-sided party bias for Pompey, as the representative of freedom, for Cato and the Republic.

---

[1] T. ii. 37; C. 353.   [2] T. ii. 82; C. 359; Mer. vi. 235.
[3] Tac. xv. 49.
[4] He wrote among other things, *saturnalia, silvæ, epigrams*, a tragedy called *Medea*; also prose works.   [5] C. 361.
[6] Hence it is not without value as an historical authority.

As a zealous Stoic, the poet exhibits an honorable, but somewhat fickle disposition, and a talent, strong and fresh, but, on account of his youth, not as yet possessing requisite moderation, and not trained to a full and even sense of form.[1] Pathetic speeches and descriptions are quite too prominent. The finest portions are the characterizations of different persons, as of Pompey and Cæsar,[2] and of Cato Uticensis.[3] The defects of the work were correctly apprehended by the ancients.[4]

Besides Lucan the following epic writers are worthy of mention: **C. Valerius Flaccus**,[5] who, under Vespasian, wrote 8 books entitled *Argonautica*, after the model of Apollonius Rhodius, correct in form, but in a style diffuse, declamatory, often artificial and obscure.

C. Silius Italicus,[6] who was born 25 A.D., was consul in 68, and lived afterwards in the most enjoyable circumstances in Campania as a man of wealth; but in 101, on account of some bodily suffering, he died a voluntary death by starvation. An ardent admirer of Virgil, but possessing only ordinary ability, Silius wrote an epic poem, in 17 books, entitled *Punica*, which contains an account of the Second Punic War up to the triumph of Scipio, with servile imitation of Homer and Virgil in style, and with a close following of Livy[7] in subject-matter.

P. Papinius Statius[8] was born about 45 A.D. at Naples, and died about 96. He was a flatterer and freedman of Do-

---

[1] C. 364.   [2] i. 129-150.   [3] ii. 380-391.
[4] Thus Quintilian (Inst. Orat. x. 1, 90) says: Lucanus ardens et concitatus et sententiis clarissimus et magis oratoribus quam poetis imitandus; and Servius, in a note on Virgil (Æn. i. 382): Lucanus videtur historiam composuisse non poema.
[5] C. 419; T. ii. 114.   [6] T. ii. 120; C. 421; Mer. vii. 222.
[7] *Maiore cura quam ingenio*, as Pliny says, Epp. iii. 7.
[8] T. ii. 123; C. 423; Mer. vii. 229; Con. i. 348.

mitian, and wrote, besides an unfinished *Achilleis* in 1½ books, a *Thebais*, in which the legend of Eteocles and Polynices is treated in a diffuse, florid, and artificial style, full of mythological learning. The *Silvæ*, as corresponding to the nature of the poet, which was suited to light versification, are far more successful and enjoyable. These consist of 32 occasional poems, in 5 books, which were thrown off in careless style,[1] and which treat of deaths, births, partings, the equestrian statue of Domitian, and the like, for the most part in epic metre, partly, also, in Alcaic, Sapphic, and Phalæcian (pendecasyllabic) metres.

Numerous attempts were made in the department of the **Didactic Epos**, as for example, by **Germanicus**,[2] the son of Drusus, who translated, with tolerable skill, the *Phænomena* of Aratus of Soli, an astronomical text-book; perhaps also by **Cæsius Bassus**,[3] a friend of Persius, and editor of his Satires, to whom a didactic poem entitled *de metris* is ascribed; furthermore, in the time of Nero originated a poem entitled *Ætna*, which treats of volcanoes, and which, made up of 645 correct hexameters, maintains a somewhat dry tone, and, in contrast to the popular belief, assumes a rationalistic standpoint in regard to myths. The author is supposed to be **Lucilius Iunior**,[4] who was imperial procurator in Sicily, and is known through his correspondence with Seneca.

c.—Satire and Fable.

Satire had, indeed, in this period, a rich and even abundant material at its service, but it could not venture upon the

---

[1] In contrast with the Thebais, a work of twelve years.
[2] T. ii. 9; C. 349.   [3] T. ii. 87; C. 356.   [4] T. ii. 95; C. 372.

political arena so long as the imperial despotism continued,[1] and it was obliged, therefore, to confine itself to literary and certain social matters. Not until the time of Trajan was the Satire allowed a greater freedom. Under the pressure of despotism, it assumed a bitter and crabbed tone, as in the cases of Persius and Juvenal; Petronius alone did not suffer his good humor to be disturbed.

The chief representatives of the Satire are given below.

A. Persius Flaccus[2] was born 34 A.D., at Volaterræ in Etruria, and was educated at Rome, chiefly by the Stoic, Annæus Cornutus. He lived only till the year 62. He possessed a morally pure mind and manner of life, was inspired with the Stoic ideal of virtue, and hence was at variance with the spirit of his times; but he lacked vivid poetic endowment and an adequate knowledge of life and reality. Persius wrote Satires which, indeed (at least, the first, in which the poetical standpoint of the author is set forth), are not without life, but which are, on the whole, only theoretical treatises on Stoic doctrines; for example, Sat. IV discusses self-knowledge; V, the true freedom of the wise man, i.e., of the Stoic; VI, life according to nature. On account of their obscure sententiousness and conciseness of language, their forced metaphors and looseness of development and connection, the Satires of Persius are very difficult of comprehension; still, they were admired even in antiquity on account of their ethical tendency, and were much read, especially in the Middle Ages.

The philosopher, **Seneca**, wrote a political Satire[3] entitled *ludus de morte Claudii* (also called *Apocolocyntosis*, — trans-

---

[1] Only against the emperor Claudius did Seneca feel himself permitted to direct his *Apocolocyntosis*.

[2] T. ii. 70; C. 355; Mer. vi. 233; Conington's Persius: Introd.

[3] C. 377; T. ii. 47; Mer. v. 463.

formation into a pumpkin), in which he again took up the form of the Satura Menippea (see p. 45). This is a venomous Satire on the apotheosis of the weak-minded emperor Claudius, by whom Seneca was banished to Corsica in the year 41. Claudius is compelled to throw dice in Heaven, always with a goblet that has no bottom, so that the dice constantly fall through; he is then given over to Caligula as a slave and spy, and finally to Menander, a freedman of Æacus. In comparison with Claudius, Nero is extolled.

The *satirical romance* of **Petronius Arbiter**[1] (originally consisting of 20 books) had also the form and character of the Satura Menippea. Of this work, however, only a series of fragments remains, in particular the *cena Trimalchionis*, a description of a feast in the house of an enormously wealthy upstart, who, though of very plebeian manners, and utterly lacking in taste and culture, yet makes a foolish exhibition of himself[2] with disgusting boastfulness. The scene of the story is laid in Lower Italy; the story itself is put in the mouth of different persons, especially of the freedman Encolpius, and hence the language varies according to the grade of culture of the speaker. The work abounds in crude and often very coarse elements; is, however, full of spirit and wit, and highly interesting as giving a knowledge of the moral and social condition of the times, as well as of the colloquial language, especially of the lower classes. According to the description of Petronius' character as given by Tacitus, it is, perhaps, not improbable that the author is identical with the C. Petronius who, according to Tacitus,[3] was the confidant and maître de plaisir of the emperor Nero, and was compelled by him to commit suicide in 66

---

[1] T. ii. 88; C. 394; Mer. vi. 164.   [3] Ann. xvi. 17, seq.
[2] Putidissima iactatio, Petr. § 73.

A.D. It is, however, more certain that the work was composed in the time of Nero.

The most important satirist of this period is **Dec. Iunius Iuvenalis**, who was born at Aquinum (about the year 50?), received rhetorical instruction at Rome, was, for a time, advocate, and also tribunus militum in Britain under Domitian, and was banished in extreme old age, probably under Hadrian, either to Egypt or Britain, ostensibly on account of an allusion to a favorite of the Emperor in Sat. VII, 90. It is probable that he died in exile.

Of Juvenal we have 16 *Satires*[1] in 5 books, arranged according to the time of their composition, which, though not written until the time of Trajan and Hadrian, treat almost entirely, so far as matters are not considered which pertain to man in general, of Romans and Roman affairs under the reign of Domitian.

Juvenal's satire[2] is an outcome of Domitian's reign of terror. The poet expresses his feeling in I, 89 : facit indignatio versum, — his indignation makes him a poet. In consequence of what he has experienced and felt, he is a pessimist in his view of mankind ; a nihilist, in respect to religion ; as a delineator of customs and as a poet, a realist, and the last, indeed, to an extreme. He portrays in its most naked hideousness the vicious society of his time, — so vicious as boldly to flaunt its vice, — with a rhetorical pathos of delineation reaching to the offensive and disgusting : yet the language is for the most part forcible, drastic, and moving, though sometimes difficult to understand.

The later satires[3] have a less passionate, more languid tone than the earlier, a fact which is explained by the increasing

---

[1] T. ii. 156; C. 442; Macleane's Commentary; Introd.; Mayor's Juvenal.
[2] C. 445; Mer. vii. 228, 273.   [3] Mer. vii. 276.

age of the poet, but which has given occasion to critics[1] for groundless and untenable doubts as to the genuineness of Satires X, XII–XV, and separate parts of other satires.

The most interesting satires are : I, the standpoint of the poet ; III, the disagreeable features of life in the metropolis ; IV, an anecdote from Domitian's time ; V, the misery of clients ; VII, the position of literary men.

The **Fable**, styled by Seneca[2] *intemptatum Romanis ingeniis opus*, was first treated as a special kind of poetry by **Phædrus**,[3] of whom nothing is known except that he was a native of Pieria, that he came to Rome as a slave, was set free by Augustus, and was persecuted under Tiberius on account of some offensive verses.

His 92 fables of animals, for the most part imitated from Æsop, and written in iambic trimeter, form 5 books. Some anecdotes are intermingled with them. They have for their object the moral improvement of the reader, yet, at the same time, they preserve a sprightly tone.[4] They are, on the whole, metrically correct, and written in fluent, if not (especially in the later books) quite pure, language. Whether the fables contained in the appendix are to be ascribed to Phædrus is doubtful.

d.—Lyric Poetry and Epigram.

Lyric Poetry was represented in this period by no important production, although the preparation of lyric poems according to set rule and pattern was a very common occu-

---

[1] Among them, O. Ribbeck.
[2] Consol. ad Polyb. 8, 27.
[3] T. ii. 32; C. 349; Mer. v. 262.
[4] Cf. prolog. to Lib. I : duplex libelli dos est : quod risum movet et quod prudenti vitam consilio monet.

pation, so that many persons considered it a duty, from time to time, perhaps every day, to produce something in verse.

Quintilian[1] mentions **Cæsius Bassus**, the friend of Persius (see p. 92) as a lyric poet. Among the best lyrics belong the *silvæ* of **Statius**[2] (see p. 91). *Erotic poems* were written by **Arruntius Stella**,[3] a friend of Statius, and **Sulpicia**,[4] the wife of Calenus, to whom is ascribed, also, a *satire* which is, without doubt, of later origin, and has often been appended to the works of Ausonius or Juvenal.

On the other hand, the **Epigram** found skilful treatment at the hands of **M. Valerius Martialis**,[5] who, born at Bilbilis in Spain about the year 40, lived chiefly at Rome in limited circumstances, although he was rewarded by Domitian for his flatteries with the ius trium liberorum and the office of tribune. About the year 98 he returned to Bilbilis, received an estate there as a present from a domina Marcella, and died in the year 102, probably at the same place.

His epigrams,[6] 1555 in all, in 14 books, together with a *liber spectaculorum*, are partly mere mottoes for presents[7] at the Saturnalia, and partly real epigrams with a designed point at the close, in which the whole effect lies. They are written in elegiac, phalæcian, and choliambic metres. Martial had a remarkable gift for seizing upon the ridiculous and piquant, and also upon the common, the ugly, and the obscene, and combining them into a short poem with endless wit and surprising turns of thought." Lessing says of him : " Only a few have made so many epi-

---

[1] Inst. Orat. x. 1, 96.
[2] T. ii. 126 ; C. 424.
[3] T. ii. 133 ; C. 425.
[4] C. 434.
[5] C. 429.
[6] T. ii. 128 ; Paley and Stone's Commentary ; Introd.
[7] For example, liber XIII, *xenia* and liber XIV, *apophoreta*.
[8] C. 432 ; Mer. vii. 231 ; Con. i. 429.

grams as Martial, and no one has made, among so many, so many good ones, and so many really excellent ones." Unfortunately, the enjoyment is not seldom destroyed for the respectable reader, both by the abjectness of mind with which Martial celebrates, importunes, and glorifies his patrons, especially Domitian, and by the ruthless wounding of the moral sense, of which he himself is well aware. The former is not justified by the poverty of his condition, nor is the latter sufficiently excused by an appeal to the taste of the public, the demands and pet fancies of his patrons, or the precedent of other poets and his own pure manner of life.

II. PROSE.

a. — History.

An objective apprehension and representation of the present and the immediate past (up to the last period of the Republic) necessarily became lost in the century of despotism; partly in consequence of the unlimited flattery, partly on account of hatred toward the government.[1] The free-thinking and free-writing historians could find no place under the Julian dynasty and Domitian. **A. Cremutius Cordus**[2] was forced to commit suicide under Tiberius. His *annales*, which treated in a liberal manner of the close of the Republic, were ordered by the enslaved senate to be burned, and yet they were widely circulated and read.[3]

The portrayal of their own times was undertaken, for the most part, by the rulers themselves. Not only **Augustus**, but also **Tiberius, Claudius,**[4] and his wife, the younger

---

[1] Libidine assentandi vel odio adversus dominantes. Tac. Hist. i. 1.
[2] T. ii. 15; C. 340; Mer. v. 182.
[3] Cf. Tac. Ann. iv. 34, seq. [4] T. ii. 9. 36; C. 352.

Agrippina, and later, **Vespasian**[1] wrote commentaries. **Aufidius Bassus** wrote, under Tiberius, a *history of the civil wars and the war against the Germans;* the elder **Pliny** continued this work, writing 20 books *bellorum Germaniæ* and 31 books *a fine Aufidii Bassi*. Also **Fabius Rusticus**,[2] who seems to have been still living in the year 108, and **Cluvius Rufus** wrote the *history of their time*. All these works have been lost. The following, however, have been preserved: —

Velleius Paterculus, tribunus militum beginning with the year 1 A.D., served under the command of Tiberius in Germany, and was made prætor on his recommendation. The year of his death is unknown. He wrote *historiæ Romanæ ad M. Vinicium cons.* (a. 30) *libri II*.[3] The introduction to the first book, and the time from the rape of the Sabine women to the war with Perseus of Macedonia, have been lost. Velleius begins with the earliest history, which, however, he throws off very summarily, paying special attention to the chronology. Afterwards the narrative becomes constantly more diffuse, only at last to empty itself into a sea of immoderate and verbose glorification of Tiberius. There is a lack of exhaustive preparatory study, the apprehension and choice of material is subjective and dilettant, induced more by interest in persons (as when he comes to speak of his commander in the war) than in things. The style is far-fetched, often inflated to the panegyric tone of the court, with an artificiality far removed from good taste. But at the same time evidences of sound judgment often appear, and there is no lack of apt and drastic characterizations.[4]

---

[1] T. ii. 100.   [2] T. ii. 100.   [3] T. ii. 17; C. 344; Mer. v. 230.
[4] For example, that of C. Marius, ii. 11; of Mithridates of Pontus, ii. 18; of Pompey, ii. 29; of Cato Uticensis, ii. 35; of Cæsar, ii. 41, and of others.

Valerius Maximus[1] was not an historian but only a compiler of notes and anecdotes. He wrote, under Tiberius, *factorum et dictorum memorabilium libri IX*, of which two compendia from the fifth and seventh centuries are extant. They were probably written as a collection of models for rhetoricians, and for the purpose of earning money. The examples, taken alternately from Roman and foreign history, are arranged according to certain topics, as *de religione, de miraculis;* according to the different virtues and vices, and the like. The treatment is in the highest degree lacking in judgment and taste, frequently even nonsensical and childish, while the style is often absurdly sprawling and needlessly pathetic. In addition to this, there occasionally appears disgusting flattery of the imperial family. At the most, some value can be ascribed to the compilation for the material it contains, though it is much too uncritical and rhetorical to be able to serve as a reliable historical authority.

Q. Curtius Rufus,[2] probably a rhetorician, wrote *historiæ Alexandri Magni libri X* (of which I and II have been lost), with close dependence upon the existing authorities, especially the Alexandrian Clitarchus. The common acceptation now is, that he wrote at the beginning of the reign of Claudius,[3] though by some he is placed under Augustus or Vespasian.

Curtius exhibits no great historical sense, and, indeed, little understanding of military affairs. Only the good fortune of Alexander is made prominent, while his importance as a statesman is not recognized. The book was intended to furnish entertaining reading, for which reason

---

[1] T. ii. 20; C. 346. [2] T. ii. 54; C. 392.
[3] The passage, x. 9, 3–6, accords best with that supposition.

special stress is laid upon what is wonderful, full of adventure, and exciting to the imagination.

As regards style, the imitation of Livy is very evident in the choice of words and phraseology. Still, the periodic sentences of Livy are, for the most part, broken up into the short, disconnected sentences with poetic coloring which were suited to the taste of that time.

Finally, Curtius is skilled in dramatic grouping and effective delineation; especially the speeches are prepared with careful attention to rhetorical rules.

Cornelius Tacitus,[1] born of a family of note, probably not after the year 54, excels all other historians either of this or of any former period. The conclusion that Interamna (now Terni) in Umbria was his birthplace has been drawn from the fact that the emperor Tacitus, who had the historian's works carefully collected, was a native of that place. But this does not prove that Tacitus was really born there any more than the fact that the citizens of Terni had a monument erected to him in the year 1514.

Tacitus pursued rhetorical studies at Rome under Marcus Aper, Iulius Secundus, perhaps, also, under Quintilian; married, in the year 78, the daughter of Iulius Agricola; filled the ordinary offices up to the prætorship under Vespasian, Titus, and Domitian; was absent from Rome (as ambassador?) in the year 90 and after; became consul under Nerva in the year 97, and died, probably in the beginning of Hadrian's reign.

His writings, arranged in chronological order, are the following: —

1. *Dialogus de oratoribus*,[2] a dialogue on the decline of oratory in the time of the emperors, which is represented as

---

[1] Schlegel: Hist. of Lit. 76; C. 449.   [2] T. ii. 172; C. 450.

occurring in the year 75, and in which Curiatius Maternus, M. Aper, Iulius Secundus, and Vipstanus Messala appear as the speakers. This dialogue was written under Domitian, and was denied by many to be the work of Tacitus on account of its style, which, in imitation of Cicero, was somewhat diffuse and florid. But the whole spirit of the production points unmistakably to Tacitus.

2. *De vita et moribus Iulii Agricolæ*,[1] written in 97 or 98, a biography of the father-in-law of Tacitus, who was governor of Britain from 78–85, and who, having been recalled by Domitian, in spite of, or rather on account of his famous deeds, died under the suspicion of poisoning, in the year 93. The biography is not really a laudatio, but is a work rhetorical in style, written in loving remembrance of Agricola.

3. *Germania*[2] (also *de situ, moribus et populis Germaniæ*), probably written in 98, and intended primarily to be simply a monographic study for a larger historical work, perhaps (if it be true that Tacitus was in Germany as an ambassador) founded upon what he himself had seen. In contrast to the corrupt condition of things at Rome, he pictures the freedom and spontaneous morality of the Germans in an ideal light, although the satirical purpose of the work may not be looked upon as the chief one. The first part (c. 1–27) treats *in commune de omnium Germanorum origine ac moribus;* the second (c. 28–46) of the separate tribes, in geographical order. This work is the chief authority in all ancient literature for our knowledge of the ancient Germans.

4. *Historiæ*,[3] originally consisting of 14 books, of which, however, only Books I–IV and a part of Book V have been

---

[1] T. ii. 174; C. 451.   [2] T. ii. 177.
[3] T. ii. 181; C. 452; Mer. vi. 372, vii. 236.

preserved. The work contained an account of the period from Galba to the death of Domitian (69–96). The extant portion embraces the year 69 and a part of 70. One of the most interesting parts is the excursus on Palestine and the Jews.[1] The work was composed under Trajan.

5. *Annales*[2] (more accurately, *ab excessu Divi Augusti liber*), in 16 books, of which, however, only Books I–IV and XII–XV have been preserved entire, V, VI, XI, and XVI in incomplete form. The work was a history of the Julian dynasty from the death of Augustus to that of Nero, to which the *Historiae* formed the chronological continuation. The years 29–31, 37–47, embracing, among other things, the entire reign of Caligula, are wanting; also, 66–68. The work was written between 115 and 117. The arrangement, though annalistic in design, still often allows the events of several years, when related to each other, to be brought together in the narration.

A projected account of the time of Augustus, to be followed by a history of the reigns of Nerva and Trajan, was never written by Tacitus.

Tacitus writes on the basis of a careful and exhaustive study of the authorities.[3] These were partly oral traditions, partly older documents and writings, such as the *acta diurna*, and perhaps also the *acta senatus*, various memoirs, as those of the younger Agrippina, the historical works of Cluvius Rufus, the elder Pliny, and others. He strives earnestly to proceed in a critical and impartial way,[4] but from the outset he holds firmly to the political opinion that

---

[1] v. 2, sqq.
[2] T. ii. 183; C. 453; Frost's commentary on the Annals; Nipperdey's Annals, translated by Browne.
[3] T. ii. 193; C. 455; Mer. vii. 238.
[4] Sine ira et studio, Ann. i. 1; fides incorrupta, Hist. i. 1.

the rule of the senate during the good old times of the Republic was the ideal one, and that the rule of the emperors is a necessary evil. Politically, therefore, he is a pronounced aristocrat and an admirer of the Republic. True, being hard pressed, he makes so much concession to the actual state of things, as to assume the position of resignation and reluctant recognition, yet he is so thoroughly embittered by despotism, and that, too, the despotism of a Domitian, under whose bloody suspicion his own relatives had to suffer, that only under the reign of a Nerva does he reluctantly acknowledge the union of *libertas* and *principatus*. Accordingly, there may be seen under all that he writes this bitter humor,[1] which causes him to doubt even concerning the government of the gods, and leads sometimes to one-sided and hypercritical judgments.[2]

On the whole, however, Tacitus earnestly endeavors to give a really adequate account by means of a thorough investigation and portrayal of the *causæ* and *rationes*, the external and internal causes and reasons of things;[3] in which attempt he displays a perfect mastery in psychological analysis and in characterization, above all in the history of Tiberius.[4] A fixed philosophical way of looking at things, taken from an existing system, Tacitus does not have. Moreover his religious views are not entirely settled and logical. He is sometimes inclined, in view of what he is compelled to see and hear, entirely to discard the thought of a divine government of the world, yet fatalistic touches

---

[1] Mer. vii. 274.

[2] This has led recent writers, especially Adolf Stahr, to the much more one-sided and partizan assertion that Tacitus is an uncritical, prejudiced writer, nay, even malicious, and a wilful distorter of the truth; and that he has in manifold ways knowingly corrupted history, with aristocratic crabbedness, especially in his account of Tiberius.

[3] Mer. vii. 234.   [4] Ann. i.-vi.

occasionally appear in spite of the psychological and objective design.

The style[1] of Tacitus still bears in the first work (*Dialogus*) a Ciceronian imprint, reminds one distinctly of Sallust in the second and third (*Agricola* and *Germania*), but he rises in the fourth and fifth (*Historiæ* and *Annales*) to a full independence. Tacitus is earnest, stately, and solemn (σεμνός), full of conscious gravity as an aristocrat, never swept away into a passionate tone, ponderous in thought, and compact in style. By his conciseness he arouses thought and imagination; he avoids the common and low, and is attracted by the extraordinary.

b.—Oratory.

In this period, as in the previous one, there was no lack of rhetorically educated men, some of whom were also active in literary work, and published orations; there were wanting, however, freedom and opportunity, courage and appreciation for public free speech. Oratory was carefully confined to the senate and the courts of the Centumviri (civil courts), which had nothing to do with politics; it was, therefore, inevitable that oratory should fall more and more into disuse.[2] The rhetorical exercises of the schools were, therefore, all the more eagerly pursued, in which the entire stress was laid upon form, expression, and style, upon ingenious and elegant turns of expression, upon witty and subtle conceits, figures, and contrasts, — in short upon everything that could

---

[1] C. 454; Frost's Annals of Tacitus: Life, etc.; Bötticher's Essay in Smith's Tacitus.

[2] This decline, most intimately connected with the political development, and the contrast between the old and the new oratory, are treated by Tacitus. dial. de orat. T. i. 385; C. 246.

produce a momentary effect.[1] The subject-matter of these rhetorical exercises can be seen from the work of the elder **Annæus Seneca**,[2] which is a very valuable contribution to the history of oratory, and is entitled *oratorum et rhetorum sententiæ, divisiones, colores*. This work, which was written not long before his death at the request of his son, contained 10 books of *controversiæ*, of which about half are preserved entire, and the rest in a compendium of later date ; also one book of *suasoriæ*, essays upon subjects discussed in the schools. The task was zealously undertaken by the author, in reliance upon his extraordinary power of memory, but in the course of his work, he himself became disgusted with it, — a sign of his good sense.

The most important rhetorician of this period, however, was **M. Fabius Quintilianus**,[3] born at Calagurris in Spain, probably while Tiberius was still on the throne ; he was appointed by Vespasian as the first salaried teacher of rhetoric in Rome, an office which he filled for twenty years ; he was afterwards called by Domitian to be the tutor of his grand-nephew, received the honors of a consul, and died about the year 98.

He was a man of noble and benevolent disposition, comprehensive learning, and cultivated and temperate judgment. The only one of his writings that has been preserved is a work written after he had retired from the office of a public teacher. It is in 12 books, entitled *institutio oratoria*, a complete introduction to the study of oratory, in which, contrary to the corrupt fashionable tone of his contempora-

---

[1] T. ii. 7.

[2] Father of the philosopher, and a native of Corduba in Spain ; he lived from about 54 B.C. to 40 A.D., mostly in Rome. T. i. 544; C. 321; Mer. iv. 432.

[3] T. ii. 320; C. 407; Mer. vii. 225.

ries (in particular of the philosopher Seneca), the writer sees in the older orators, especially Cicero, the ideal of an orator. Book I treats of the preparatory grammatical studies; II, of the elements and essence of rhetoric; III–VII, of *inventio* and *dispositio*; VIII–XI, of *elocutio*, together with *memoria* and *pronuntiatio*: XII describes the finished orator. The tenth book is especially interesting, since it contains a parallel view and characterization of the most important Greek and Roman poets and prose authors.

One of the most learned pupils of Quintilian was **C. Plinius Cæcilius Secundus**,[1] commonly called the younger Pliny. He was born at Novum Comum (Como) in the year 62, became consul in the year 100, was governor of Bithynia 111–112, and died, doubtless soon after his return to Rome.

He was an advocate of very wide practice. Of his speeches we still possess the *panegyricus*,[2] a eulogy on Trajan in return for the gift of the consulship. The speech is much injured by the strongly-exaggerated praise which it contains, the pompous studiedness of its style, and its diffuse rhetoric. Much more attractive and interesting are his *Epistulæ*,[3] in 9 Books,[4] which he wrote with a view to publication during the years 96–109,[5] and afterwards actually published. These letters, from the fact that they were intended for publication, come very far, it is true, from making the fresh impression of immediateness characteristic of Cicero's letters; one sees clearly that the smooth, uniform style is not a product of the moment; yet they give us a very valuable and varied picture of that period, espe-

---

[1] T. ii. 187; C. 437. [2] T. ii. 192; Mer. vii. 439.
[3] T. ii. 190; C. 439; Mer. vii. 250; Church and Brodribb's Pliny: Introd.
[4] Exclusive of his correspondence with Trajan.
[5] Possibly 96–111 or 112.

cially of the often frivolous literary activity, and show us the writer as a man not at all genial, indeed, and even vain and pedantic, yet well-meaning, and humane even to tenderness, very eager to learn and to know, interesting himself in everything, striving sincerely for the good and the beautiful. A separate book is formed by the correspondence between Trajan and Pliny, during the governorship of the latter in Bithynia, in which, especially, the letters (96, 97) relating to the treatment of the Christians are valuable. Book VI, 16, contains a description of the eruption of Vesuvius in the year 79.

Concerning Tac. *dialogus de oratoribus*, see p. 101.

c. — Philosophy.

Philosophy found in this period, as in the preceding one, not a few disciples. They were, however, for the most part, dilettanti, who treated philosophical subjects without exhaustive study and without logical system. The majority in these troublous times inclined to Stoicism, especially men who were opposed to the government.[1] At the same time, exaggeration and ostentation were sometimes carried to extremes. The great number of Greek philosophers who flooded Rome brought philosophy into disrepute, and caused Vespasian and Domitian to banish them from Italy.

By far the most important philosophical writer is **L. Annæus Seneca**,[2] born about the year 4 A.D. at Corduba in Spain, son of Seneca the rhetorician (see p. 106). He was educated at Rome, became senator, was banished by Claudius to Corsica in the year 41 at the instigation of Messalina, was recalled in the year 49 at the request of

---

[1] For example, Pætus Thrasea, Lucan, Persius, Helvidius Priscus, and others. [2] T. ii. 40; C. 378; Ritter, iv. 174; Farrar: Seekers after God.

Agrippina, became tutor of Nero, was consul in 57, and, in the year 65, was compelled by Nero to commit suicide by opening his veins in a bath, on a charge of participation in the conspiracy of Piso.

Not always living up to the teachings of the Stoa,[1] to which he subscribed in the main, and free, neither in his life nor in his writings, from vanity and striving after effect, Seneca nevertheless sought as far as possible to exercise a healthful influence, and showed not only a rare versatility of talent, an uncommon wealth of thought, a fine faculty of observation, and a sound, practical mind, keeping itself free from the exaggerations of the Stoics, but also, for that time and society, a surprising loftiness of moral view.[2] In this he outstrips his time, inasmuch as he both abandons that which is specifically Roman and adopts a cosmopolitan humanity; for which reason, Christian tradition has even made him a Christian and a friend of the apostle Paul.

Seneca's style,[3] the antipodes of the Ciceronian,[4] is forced and ornamental, according to the taste of the period. It moves, for the most part, in brief, disconnected, and often paradoxical sentences and phrases and piquant antitheses. The same thought is forever varied, ingeniously indeed, but not seldom to weariness.

Of Seneca's writings, which are preserved only in part, some are poetical,[5] some prosaic, and some of the latter,

---

[1] This is shown by the fact that he had great wealth, was indulgent toward Nero's sensuality (of necessity, it is true, and to avoid something worse), and that he excused the murder of Agrippina.

[2] C. 382; Mer. vi. 112, 231; Ritter, iv. 180.

[3] T. ii. 42; C. 300; Mer. vii. 225; Ritter, iv. 175.

[4] According to Quintilian, Inst. Orat. x. 1, 129: *abundans dulcibus vitiis*, and according to Caligula's correct comparison, Suet. Calig. 53: *arena sine calce*.

[5] *Tragœdiæ* (see p. 89). Also a part of the *Apocolocyntosis* (see p. 93) is in poetry.

again, relate to natural science,[1] and some to morals.[2] Of most general interest are the 124 *Epistulæ ad Lucilium*[3] (see p. 92), written, like Pliny's epistles, with a view to publication; they are, in reality, popular treatises, containing an abundance of apt observations and rules of morals, as well as many characteristic features of life at that time. A correspondence with the apostle Paul (14 letters), ascribed to Seneca[4] by the church-father Hieronymus (about 400), is not genuine, but rests on the correct perception that the moral views of Seneca are often allied to those of Christianity in a surprising degree.

d.—Special Sciences.

The most important points respecting the special sciences in this period are the following:—

In **Law**, Capito (see p. 84) was followed by **Masurius Sabinus**,[5] who lived from Tiberius to Nero, and was the author of a much commentated work, *libri III iuris civilis*. Labeo was followed by the somewhat later **Sempronius Proculus**. The two schools were commonly called, after these men, the Sabinian[6] and the Proculian.[7] Both schools had distinguished literary representatives.

The **Science of Language** became more and more an object of study in connection with Rhetoric. Many of the emperors took a lively interest in it. **Claudius** had under consideration a reform of the alphabet, and wished to intro-

---

[1] *Naturales quæstiones libri III*, used as a text-book in physics in the Middle Ages.

[2] For example, *de ira libri III, de beneficiis libri VII*, several *consolationes, de tranquillitate animi*, and others. T. ii. 46; C. 379.

[3] T. ii. 45; C. 385.   [4] T. ii. 48; C. 386; Mer. vi. 230.   [5] T. ii. 27.

[6] Also Cassian, from **Cassius Longinus**, a pupil of Sabinius.

[7] Hadley's Introd. to Roman Law, 63.

duce three new letters.[1] Vespasian appointed Quintilian as teacher of philology.

The following writers were distinguished as **grammarians and commentators:** —

Q. Remmius Palæmo,[2] from Vicenza, the author (under Claudius) of a *grammar* which was much used; **Q. Asconius Pedianus**,[3] who wrote under Claudius, Nero, and Vespasian, and from whom we have *commentaries* on five of Cicero's orations (among them, *pro Milone*), containing valuable material, but not preserved entire; **M. Valerius Probus**[4] of Berytus, about the year 60, a critical commentator, especially of the Roman classic poets; under Domitian, **Æmilius Asper**;[5] under Trajan, **Flavius Caper**[6] and **Velius Longus**, from both of whom works *de orthographia* are preserved.

Among **mathematical writers**, the land surveyors, agrimensores, or gromatici,[7] are worthy of special mention. Of these the most distinguished were **Sex. Iulius Frontinus**[8] and **Hyginus**.[9] Frontinus, born about the year 40, was consul three times, served as general in Gaul, Britain, and Germany, was curator aquarum in 67, and died about 103. Of his works on surveying only extracts are preserved. As curator aquarum he wrote a work entitled *de aquis urbis Romæ libri II*, which is valuable for the information it contains. Hyginus wrote under Trajan a work on surveying which has been preserved only in fragments. Both were also writers on *military subjects*, Frontinus, as

---

[1] Ⅎ = consonantal *v*, Ↄ antisigma, for *bs* and *ps*, Ⱶ representing an intermediate sound between *i* and *u*. T. ii. 38; C. 11.
[2] T. ii. 29; C. 348.
[3] T. ii. 62; C. 393.
[4] T. ii. 73; C. 394.
[5] T. ii. 151; C. 412.
[6] T. ii. 209; C. 442.
[7] From *groma*, a measuring-staff.
[8] T. ii. 147; C. 410.
[9] T. ii. 203; C. 442.

author of a lost work on *tactics*, and an extant one of *strategemata* (military stratagems), in 3 books, together with a fourth, *strategematica*, as a supplement; Hyginus, as author of a work entitled *de munitionibus*, and perhaps also of another, *de limitibus*.

In the department of **Geography**, may be mentioned **Pomponius Mela**,[1] from Tingentera in Spain, author of the oldest Roman description of the world that has come down to us. He wrote under Claudius, after older written authorities, 3 books entitled *de situ orbis* (or *de chorographia*). To geographical literature belong also, wholly or in part, the *Germania* and *Agricola* of Tacitus, the *Naturales Quaestiones* of Seneca, and especially Books III–VI of the *Naturalis Historia* of **C. Plinius Secundus**[2] (the elder Pliny). He was born in the year 23 at Novum Comum, served in the year 45 in Germany, was afterwards imperial procurator in Spain, was employed by Vespasian as an efficient officer in the financial and marine department, and perished on the 24th of August, 79, during an eruption of Vesuvius, as a sacrifice to his scientific zeal.[3] He was the uncle of the younger Pliny, and the most industrious and learned man of his time.[4] Besides his historical works (see p. 99), and his writings on tactics, grammar, and rhetoric,[5] which have not come down to us, he wrote the extant work, *Naturalis Historia*,[6] in 37 books, an encyclopædia of natural science, embracing *astronomy, geography, anthropology, zoölogy, botany, mineralogy*, and many departments of *medicine*. This encyclopædia, written with the aid of the works of nearly

---

[1] T. ii. 64, i. 77; C. 394.
[2] T. ii. 102; C. 400.
[3] Cf. Plin. Epp. vi. 16; Mer. vii. 58.
[4] Mer. vi. 187; vii. 264.
[5] As, for example, *de iaculatione equestri, dubii sermonis libri VIII, studiosi libri III.*
[6] T. i. 72, ii. 104; C. 404; Mer. vii. 226.

five hundred writers, representing nearly 2000 volumes, is an exceedingly rich mine of curiosities, and contains almost everything worth knowing, though, to be sure, it is often enough crudely put together, and without the critical care which could be desired. Since an abundance of material was of foremost importance to the author, the style [1] is, for the most part, dry, and at times also marked by rhetorical artificiality. It is lofty in those places where the greatness and majesty of nature and the universe are set forth, though Pliny stands in opposition to the popular belief in the gods.

Of the encyclopædic work of **Cornelius Celsus**,[2] written in the time of Tiberius, there are still extant 8 books *de medicina* (*de re medica*), including surgery.[3] In the same work, the *science of war, agriculture, rhetoric*, and *practical philosophy* were also treated. Inferior, from a scientific and literary point of view, is the collection of prescriptions (*compositiones medicamentorum*) of **Scribonius Largus**,[4] private physician of the emperor Claudius. Of these prescriptions, 271 are extant.

Agriculture, as such, was treated by **Moderatus Columella**[5] of Gades, a contemporary and countryman of Seneca, in his work *de re rustica libri XII*. The production bears witness to the author's technical knowledge, candid disposition, and good taste. Of this work, Book X. concerning gardening, is written in heroic metre, after the example of Virgil, though by no means equal to the model.

---

[1] T. ii. 107; C. 406.
[2] T. ii. 25; C. 347.
[3] T. i. 74.
[4] T. ii. 60; C. 393.
[5] T. i. 73, ii. 57; C. 392.

FIFTH PERIOD.

The Later Empire, after the Death of Trajan, 117 a.d.

THIS period is a time of continual decline, both in politics and literature.[1] The capacity for original and independent production, which, up to this time, had appeared at least in individual cases, ceases entirely. In its place, we find uncertainty, perversity, and dulness of judgment and taste, a slavish and unintelligent imitation of earlier and especially archaic writers, an affected and distorted style, an artificial rhetoric, dressed out with wordy ornamentation, but wanting any important inner significance answering to the lavish use of outward means. Instead of independent production, there appears a boastful and ostentatious display of pedantic and often laboriously-gathered knowledge.

The corruption of taste shows itself, especially, in the archaistic tendency, which places the classic standard authors below the ante-classic writers. The chief representative of this tendency is the rhetorician Fronto. As a consequence of the intellectual barrenness and tameness, and also of the persistent advance of Greek sophism and rhetoric, which found high favor and abundant reward in the cultured circles,[2] poetry comes to occupy a less prominent position than prose.

The provinces become more and more important in the

---

[1] T. ii. 205, 337.
[2] Especially with a number of the emperors, as Hadrian, Antoninus Pius, and Marcus Aurelius.

department of literature. A number of writers, especially Christian writers, spring up in Africa. Their latinity is characterized by a want of logical accuracy, by intemperateness of expression, rhetorical overloading, and an arbitrary construction of words and sentences. Moreover, Gaul, expecially Lugdunum (Lyon), becomes an important seat of rhetorical instruction.

Whereas the earlier emperors of this period, as Hadrian and Marcus Aurelius, and also Alexander Severus, took a lively interest in literature, it was compelled, in consequence of the political confusion of the third century, to retire into the background.

Not until after the triumph of Christianity, and the reconstruction of the empire by Constantine the Great, did more important writers, Christian as well as Pagan, appear. Meanwhile, the specifically Roman character was steadily dying out, especially since, by the edict of Caracalla, which extended the right of Roman citizenship to the provinces, universal equality was being furthered through the agency of the state. Literary production took refuge, partly in the bosom of the Christian church, and thus became the property of the Christian clergy[1] (patristic literature), partly at the court, where, without free, ideal movement, it was compelled to yield itself to the service of special, practical ends, particularly the glorification of the emperors (panegyric literature), and the extension of legal learning. This period, if one considers at the same time content and form, produced scarcely a writer of the first or even of the second rank; on the other hand, in the special sciences, particularly in the Department of Jurisprudence, important, and in some respects great and standard work, was done.

---

[1] T. ii. 468.

I. POETRY.

a.—Lyric.

Lyric poetry is represented in this period by only a few names worthy of mention. Of uncertain date is the *Pervigilium Veneris*,[1] a glorification of Venus Genetrix and of Spring, in 93 well-constructed trochaic septenarii. Half lyric, half epic, are the poems of **Dec. Magnus Ausonius**[2] of Burdigala (Bordeaux), in Gaul; a poet of fine parts, and especially successful in the form of his verse. He was a teacher of the emperor Gratianus, became consul in 379, and was converted to Christianity, though he made little use of it in his writings. In his later years, he lived under Theodosius I in his native place, absorbed in literary pursuits. His poems are very varied in form and content; *epigrams* and *epistles; poems on living and deceased persons; on emperors and celebrated cities*. His *idylls* are best known, and among these, the tenth, entitled *Mosella*, a description of a journey on the Moselle, from Bingen to Trier, in 683 hexameters, charming on account of the variedness of its contents, and the sensitive appreciation of nature displayed in it.

Among poets specifically Christian, special mention should be made of **Aurelius Prudentius Clemens**,[3] who was born in Spain in 348, was a rhetorician and high official, and died about the year 410. He composed *odes in praise of the martyrs*, and *hymns* in Horatian metres; also *dogmatic, polemic*, and *epic poems*.

---

[1] T. ii. 247; C. 468.
[2] T. ii. 385.
[3] T. ii. 431; Trench, 121; Schaff: History of the Christian Church, iii. 594; Ozonam: Civilization in the Fifth Century, ii. 196.

b.—Epic.

Epic poetry in this period is partly mythological, partly employed for panegyrics,—poems in praise of emperors and other persons in high standing, together with corresponding depreciation of their opponents. **Claudius Claudianus**[1] of Alexandria is, for his time, a brilliant representative of both styles. He composed, about the year 400, numerous *poems*, some on *historical subjects*,[2] some on *mythological*,[3] also *epistles, idylls*, and *epigrams*, mostly in elegiac metre. There appears everywhere great skill in the treatment of the form, vivid imagination, extended acquaintance with the classic poets, and enthusiasm for the greatness of Rome ; but these excellences are dimmed and injured in their effect by the insignificance of the material, which the poet endeavors in vain to conceal and make good by rhetorical exaggeration.

Less important than the pagan Claudianus are the Christian poets : —

C. Vettius Aquilius Iuvencus,[4] Spanish presbyter in the time of Constantine the Great, and author of a *New Testament History* in hexameters ; **Flavius Merobaudes**,[5] Spanish rhetorician, and author of a *poem on Christ*, and of *historical poems in praise*, especially, *of the commander, Ætius ;* **Apollinaris Sidonius**[6] (about 430–488), from Lugdunum, bishop of Clermont, and writer of *panegyrics on several of the emperors*, abounding in pedantic phrase-

---

[1] T. ii. 438 ; Ozonam, i. 170.
[2] For example, poems in praise of the emperor Honorius, and especially of Stilicho, with attacks upon the minister Rufinus and the eunuch Eutropius in Constantinople. The poems are written without any essential warping of the facts.
[3] Three books *de raptu Proserpinæ*.
[4] T. ii. 346.   [5] T. ii. 490.   [6] T. ii. 499

ology; **Dracontius**[1] of Carthage, author of *mythological epics*, also of a didactic poem, *de deo*, and others; **Venantius Fortunatus**,[2] in the sixth century, bishop of Poitiers, and writer of an *epic in honor of St. Martin of Tours*, and numerous *poems in praise of persons in high standing*.

c.—Didactic.

In **Didactic and Descriptive Poetry**, the following names are worthy of mention: **Nemesianus**[3] of Carthage (about 280), writer of a didactic poem on hunting entitled *Cynegetica*; **Festus Avienus**[4] (about 370), writer of *poems on astronomical, historical*, and especially *geographical subjects*; particularly, however, **Claudius Rutilius Namatianus**,[5] a native of Gaul, who was præfectus urbi in 414, and who, in 416, described his homeward sea-voyage from Rome to Gaul[6] in a charming style, ornamented with numerous episodes of a descriptive and personal character. The poet is an enthusiastic adherent of ancient Rome[7] and the old Pagan religion, and a decided enemy of Jews[8] and Christians.[9]

---

[1] T. ii. 519. [2] T. ii. 563; Trench, 131; Schaff, iii. 595.
[3] T. ii. 308. [4] T. ii. 382. [5] T. ii. 470.
[6] *De reditu suo libri II*, of which the second book has not been preserved entire.

[7] Cf. i. 47-164; especially verse 53, seq:
    Obruerint citius scelerata oblivia solem,
    Quam tuus ex nostro corde recedat honos.
and 81, seq:
    Omnia perpetuo quæ servant sidera motu,
    Nullum viderunt pulchrius imperium.

[8] i. 397, seq:
    Latis excisæ pestis contagia serpunt
    Victoresque suos natio victa premit.

[9] i. 525, seq:
    Non rogo deterior Circeis secta venenis?
    Tunc mutabantur corpora, nunc animi.

A collection of **Fables**, afterwards much used as a school-book, is that of **Avianus**,[1] who, about the year 400, reproduced 42 Æsopian fables in elegiac verse, after the model of Æsop, Babrius, Phædrus, and others.

II. PROSE.

a. — Oratory.

Rhetoric, with **Cornelius Fronto**[2] as its most able and illustrious representative, stood for a long time foremost in the estimation of the public. Fronto was born at Cirta in Africa, lived about 100–175, became consul in 143, was the teacher and friend of the emperor Marcus Aurelius. He was affectionate (φιλόστοργος) and sincere in disposition, in his literary efforts and productions the type of a period spending itself in complacent speechifying. Of his writings we possess some *works on rhetorical subjects*, and also some *letters*,[3] the latter, for the most part, unimportant in subject-matter.

Fronto lays all the stress upon rhetoric, to be sure, with a sincere belief in it alone as a saving power. In respect to language, Fronto is a worshipper of the most ancient ante-classical writers and orators, — of Plautus, Ennius, Cato, C. Gracchus, — and also of Sallust. He recognizes Cicero with reluctance.[4] With him, as we have said, the entire value lies in rhetorical ornamentation (εἰκόνες, verba

---

[1] T. ii. 462. [2] T. i. 58, ii. 229; C. 463; Mer. vii. 460.
[3] Correspondence with Marcus Aurelius, L. Verus, Antoninus Pius and *ad amicos;* also letters in Greek.
[4] For example, he characterizes the orators thus, *ad Verum Imperat:* Contionatur Cato infeste, Gracchus turbulente, Tullius copiose; in iudiciis sævit Cato, triumphat Cicero, tumultuatur Gracchus, Calvus rixatur.

notabilia, deminutiva, and the like). But just this artificiality and corruption of taste seemed to his contemporaries the highest excellence.

Another distinguished African rhetorician was **L. Apuleius**[1] of Madaura, born about 125, who was, at one time and another, active in many places as a rhetorician and an advocate, and was also celebrated as a magician. As a writer, he was very versatile, productive, and pretentious; his style is original, full of needless word-coinings and strange distortions of sentences, bombastic and overloaded, yet of a drastic vividness and not without pleasing humor. The best known of his writings is the fantastic romance, *Metamorphoseon libri XI*,[2] which contains the experiences of a man who was changed by magic arts into an ass, together with many stories of robbers and necromancy, of which Thessaly is most frequently the scene, all ending in the glorification of the Isis mysteries. The whole is imitated from the Λούκιος of Lucian, only it is carried much further, and changes are made that are not always fortunate. Books IV-VI contain the well-known (allegoric?) legend of Amor and Psyche. Of the remaining writings of Apuleius, the following deserve to be mentioned: *Apologia*, a defence against the charge of necromancy, written in a comparatively simple style; and *Florida*, an anthology of orations and declamations.

As a rhetorician of the later time, may be mentioned **Q. Aurelius Symmachus** the Younger,[3] consul in 391, of whom we possess 9 *orations* (not one, however, in complete form), some of which were delivered in the Senate, and some were panegyrics on the emperor Valentinian I and Gratian. We also have a collection of *epistles* in 10 books,

---

[1] T. ii. 257; C. 469.   [2] T. ii. 261; C. 471.   [3] T. ii. 397.

composed after the model of the younger Pliny, in which the letters of the tenth book are the most interesting, wherein Symmachus, in the year 384, intercedes with the emperor Valentinian II for the restoration of the altar of Victoria to the Roman curia, whence it had been removed at the command of Gratian;—that is, he interested himself in the maintainance of heathen worship,—an endeavor which was not successful, serving only to call out several controversial writings on the side of the Christians; for example, from Bishop Ambrosius of Milan.

b.—Philosophy.

Although philosophy was opposed by rhetoricians like Fronto, yet it was furthered by several emperors, especially by the Antonines, and in the person of the strict Stoic, **Marcus Aurelius,**[1] who wrote in the Greek language 12 books of *Self-Examinations* (εἰς αὑτόν), even attained to the imperial throne. Nevertheless, it could no longer develop a strong and healthy life; it degenerated often into obscure mysticism and vain love of the marvellous, as in the case of **Apuleius** (see p. 120) who wrote philosophical books *de mundo, de deo Socratis,* and others.

In Christianity, there grew up against this a new and vigorous opponent, which, indeed, often made use of the weapons of pagan philosophy and rhetoric. By this opposition many energetic spirits were spurred on to the attempt of renewing philosophy, among them **Anicius Manlius Torquatus Severinus Boëtius,**[2] the son-in-law of Symmachus, (see p. 120) consul in 510, and executed in 525 at the command of the Ostrogothic king Theodoric, on the charge of

---

[1] Farrar: Seekers after God, 303; Mer. vii. 490; T. i. 69.
[2] T. ii. 525; Milman's Latin Christianity, i. 443.

traitorous connections with the court of Constantinople. Although a Christian, he was enthusiastic for classical antiquity, a translator of many works, particularly those of Aristotle. He wrote *mathematical, grammatical*, and other works, but he is chiefly known through his *de consolatione*, composed in prison, and testifying in somewhat involved, yet easily intelligible language, written alternately in prose and verses of various metres, to a mind morally refined, permeated much more by the spirit of ancient philosophy, especially of Plato, than by that of Christianity. Also, theological writings, as, for example, a work on the Trinity, are incorrectly ascribed to Boëtius.

c.—History.

There were numerous writers of history in this period, but the freedom of thought and word necessary for a lofty flight was wanting; the influence of rhetoric asserted itself in this department of literature as in all others.[1] In place of objective arrangement and choice of material, of psychological treatment, of broad and comprehensive views, appeared an undue attention to what was merely personal, a biographical treatment of history, with an uncritical preference for the insignificant and for anecdotes, and an enumeration of details not seldom amounting to frivolity. The ancient historians were made accessible and enjoyable to the taste of the public through compendia. With the triumph of Christianity, historical writing turned its attention more and more to biblical and ecclesiastical matters.

C. Suetonius Tranquillus,[2] born about the year 75, wrote a part of his works as far back as the reign of Trajan. He was a rhetorician and an advocate; for a long time, also,

---

[1] T. i. 46.   [2] T. ii. 210; C. 457.

private secretary of the emperor Hadrian, who, however, dismissed him, whereupon he devoted himself to study and authorship in the most widely-separated departments, *history of civilization, science of language, chronology*, and the like. From his writings [1] have been preserved fragments of the work *de viris illustribus*, concerning literary celebrities of Rome up to the time of Domitian; among these fragments the *vitæ* of Terence and Horace are important, but especially the *vita* Cæsarum,[2] written in 120, consisting of biographies of the first twelve emperors, from Cæsar (the beginning of whose reign seems, however, to be wanting) to Domitian. This work is very valuable in subject-matter, carefully composed, with an extensive use of authorities, and a striving after objectivity. In consequence, however, of the interest attaching to the subject-matter itself, anecdotes and personalities prevail; also things insignificant and low are not passed by unnoticed, and in view of the division of the subject according to certain headings (such as faults, virtues, outward habits, and the like), the chronological order, as well as the inner connection, and especially the psychological arrangement, are neglected. The language is simple, natural, and easily understood.[3]

The following historians stand at a considerable distance below Suetonius: —

Florus[4] wrote, probably under Hadrian, *bellorum omnium annorum DCC libri II*, Roman history from Romulus to Augustus, arranged, generally, according to the wars, without strict chronology, and with many errors as to matters of fact. Anachronisms, not to say designed falsifications, appear, and, worst of all, a tasteless and artificial teleology *in*

---

[1] T. ii. 214; C. 459. [2] Mer. vii. 248. [3] C. 460.
[4] Possibly identical with the poet and rhetorician, P. Annius Florus. T. ii. 216; C. 462.

maiorem gloriam populi Romani. At the same time, he betrays a complete lack of historical insight and psychological apprehension. The style is rhetorically overloaded, full of stereotyped words and phrases, sometimes, however, in clear moments, picturesque and to the point.

A certain **L. Ampelius**,[1] otherwise unknown, wrote under Antoninus Pius, a dry encyclopædic manual, entitled *liber memorialis*, on geographical, mythological, and especially historical subjects.

We possess only fragments of the work of his contemporary, **Granius Licinianus**, who wrote an *outline of Roman history*. The writings of **Marius Maximus**[2] are entirely lost. He wrote, about the year 230, *biographies of the emperors* from Nerva to Heliogabalus, and was much used by later writers, especially by the **scriptores historiæ Augustæ**,[3] some of whom, as Ælius Spartianus, Volcacius Gallicanus, and Trebellius Pollio, wrote under Diocletian, and some, as Flavius Vopiscus, Ælius Lampridius, and Iulius Capitolinus, under Constantine the Great. Their work (it is uncertain when and by whom it was collected) contained the *biographies of the emperors*, from Hadrian to Numerian (117–284), written in monotonous style, in halting language, moving on generally in short sentences, without a proper separation of the important and the insignificant, and without an arrangement suited to the subject. Nevertheless, it is very valuable for the history of this period on account of the lack of other authorities. The authorship of all the biographies is not certain; the most are by Spartianus and Vopiscus.

Several works bear the name of **Aurelius Victor**,[4] who was governor of Pannonia under Theodosius the Great: *de*

---

[1] T. ii. 239; C. 468. [2] T. ii. 296. [3] T. ii. 320. [4] T. ii. 370.

Cæsaribus, from Cæsar to Constantine, an uncritical collection of material in an excessively compact style; also an *epitome de Cæsaribus*, which deviates in many ways from the original, and extends further, reaching to the time of Theodosius the Great; moreover, it depends upon other authorities, and, on the whole, is more easily understood than the de Cæsaribus. Both productions are, perhaps, compendia of a larger work of Aurelius Victor. Of unknown authorship are two other writings, which likewise bear his name: *de viris illustribus*, covering the period from Procas to Cleopatra, and written with general good sense; and *origo gentis Romanæ*, from Saturn to the death of Romulus, a silly production having not the least value.

To the same time with Aurelius Victor belongs **Eutropius**,[1] who wrote, under Valens, a *breviarium historiæ Romanæ*, in 10 books, covering the period from the foundation of Rome to the time of Jovian. It is, in general, unpretentious and true to facts; but, in the earlier books, it is dry and betrays a total neglect of the inner relations of things; in depicting the time of the emperors, however, it is fuller and fresher, containing many good characterizations.[2] The work was afterwards much used as a school-book.

The work of **Ammianus Marcellinus**[3] is valuable as an historical authority. He was born in Antiochia; after long service in the army, he wrote, about the year 390, at Rome, 31 books *rerum gestarum*, in which the period from Nerva to Valens was described. Only Books XIV–XXXI are extant, embracing the time 353–376. Ammianus, as an enthusiastic worshipper of Julian the Apostate, writes from

---

[1] T. ii. 372.
[2] For example, that of Trajan, viii. 4; that of Constantine the Great, x. 7; that of Julian, x. 16.
[3] T. ii. 407.

a pagan standpoint with impartiality and fidelity to the truth. His intentions are honorable and his judgment good, and he often writes from a recollection of what he himself has seen and experienced. His style, on the contrary, is forbidding and unenjoyable on account of its excessive condensation and affectation. This was the result of wide reading without proper digestion, of an attempt to utilize his extensive collection of notes, and of an unripe half-culture, comprehending least of all the spirit of the Latin language.

Works were written from the standpoint of Christianity by the Aquitanian presbyter **Sulpicius Severus**[1] (about 400), and his contemporary, the Spanish presbyter **Orosius**,[2] who wrote *outlines of universal history*, from Adam down to their time. Both works are without special value. Further, **Magnus Aurelius Cassiodorius**[3] (-orus?), who lived from 480 to 575, and was private secretary of Theodoric, and in the year 540 and afterwards was in the Bruttian monastery, Viviers, wrote a *chronicle from Adam down to 519 A.D.;* also, *a history of the Goths*, preserved, unfortunately, only in the scanty epitome of the Goth **Iordanis**[4] (about 550); and 12 books *variarum*, a collection of official documents, as well as numerous *theological* and *encyclopædic works*.

The Briton **Gildas**[5] wrote, in the sixth century, a *History of Britain*, from 449 A.D.; and a *History of the Kingdom of the Franks* was written by **Gregorius** of Tours (Bishop in 573 and afterwards) with a mind open to historical truth, in spite of his orthodox prejudices.

An important authority for the statistics of the later Roman Empire are the official state records, written at the close of

---

[1] T. ii. 448.
[2] T. ii. 472.
[3] T. ii. 539.
[4] T. ii. 547.
[5] T. ii. 549.

the fourth century, and entitled. *Notitia dignitatum et administrationum omnium tam civilium quam militarium in partibus orientis et occidentis.*[1]

d.—Special Sciences.

Among the special sciences, that of **Law**[2] occupies the foremost place. From the outset a national Roman science, it attained its highest development under the emperors, from Hadrian's time to about the year 230. Civil law was admirably set forth by the eminent jurists, who lived, for the most part, at the imperial court, and were held in great esteem, while their opinions, decisions (*responsa*), and manuals became standard in the administration of justice. Thus, after legal productions ceased about the middle of the third century, there arose in their place, in the fourth century, an active zeal for collecting and codifying the existing legal authorities.

The most important jurists are given below: **Salvius Iulianus**,[3] aside from independent works, compiled and published, under Hadrian, in the year 131, the so-called *Edictum perpetuum*. This was a collection of opinions of the Roman prætors, from the time of the Republic, and a weighty legal authority in later times. His contemporary, **Sex. Pomponius**, was the author of numerous works, which were afterwards much used. The four books *Institutionum* (introduction to the science of law), which were written by **Gaius**[4] about the year 160, and are, in great part, preserved, were much used as a text-book. They became the basis of the Institutions of Justinian. Two other very

---

[1] T. i. 78.
[2] Sandars' Justinian: Introd. 20, Am. Ed.; T. i. 64; Hadley.
[3] T. ii. 219; C. 462.   [4] T. ii. 244; C. 466; Hadley, 71.

important jurists were **Æmilius Papinianus**[1] and **Domitius Ulpianus**.[2] The former, præfectus prætorio under Septimius Severus, and afterwards executed by command of Caracalla, was the author of much-used *responsa* and *quæstiones*. He was distinguished by great breadth of views, independence of apprehension, and strong moral sensibility. Ulpianus, a native of Tyre, præfectus prætorio under Alexander Severus, and assassinated in 228, was the author of numerous writings, which are much cited in the Justinian Digests. **Iulius Paulus**,[3] a contemporary of Ulpianus, was active in the same line, and his writings were much used, especially in the Pandects of Justinian. **Herennius Modestinus**,[4] a pupil of Ulpianus, may also be mentioned.

Among the collections of those constitutions which originated during the time from Hadrian to Diocletian, the first was the **Codex Gregorianus**,[5] which was begun by a jurist Gregorianus; then followed the **Codex Hermogenianus** in the last part of the reign of Constantine the Great, and, at the same time, the **Fragmenta Vaticana**.[6] About a hundred years later (438) appeared the **Codex Theodosianus**,[7] which contained, in 16 books, the constitutions that had been published under Constantine the Great, and which was afterwards the standard in the eastern empire until the Codex of Justinian. Finally, the key-stone of this imposing legal structure was the **Corpus Iuris**,[8] which was prepared in the reign of Justinian by a commission of jurists, at whose head stood Tribonianus. The separate parts of this Corpus Iuris are as follows: The **Codex Iustinianeus** of the year

---

[1] T. ii. 268; Hadley, 11.
[2] T. ii. 283; Hadley, 10.
[3] T. ii. 287.
[4] T. ii. 289.
[5] T. ii. 325.
[6] T. ii. 348.
[7] T. ii. 485.
[8] T. ii. 553; Hadley, 3; Sandars, 23; Milman's Latin Christianity, i. 484.

529; the **Institutiones**, taking the place of the original Cod. Iust., in 533; the **Digesta**, or **Pandects**,[1] and an enlarged edition of the Cod. Iust. from the year 534. To these were added, after the death of Justinian, three private collections, **Novellæ**, written mostly in Greek. This Corpus Iuris made the earlier writings superfluous by absorbing them, so far as their essential contents were concerned, established the final stability and uniformity of law, and served ever after as a foundation for its later unfolding and development.

Of the remaining special sciences, **Philology** and **Archæology**[2] were most cultivated. Under Hadrian, Antoninus Pius, and Marcus Aurelius, the learned men in this department, especially those of Fronto's school, were highly respected and well paid. Nevertheless, independence, certainty, and correctness of judgment began to disappear, and the process of making compendia and plundering from older works was carried on more widely, yet often without taste and critical care, with the one-sided, more or less perfunctory purpose of accumulating materials and getting a collection of notes. The outcome of this activity was, partly encyclopædic collections and compilations of all kinds of antiquarian notes, partly elementary books on grammar, metre, orthography, lexicography, and partly commentaries on the earlier poets, particularly Virgil.

The following names are especially worthy of mention: —

1. **Compilers: Aulus Gellius**,[3] born about 130, studied in Athens, and lived afterwards in Rome. He made it his life-work to make compilations from the older writers, and he put the results of his long, industrious studies into the

---

[1] Excerpts from the most distinguished jurists, in 50 books.
[2] T. i. 51.   [3] T. ii. 254; C. 465.

20 books *Noctes Atticæ*,[1] which (except Book VIII) are extant, and embrace *language, literature, jurisprudence, philosophy*, and *natural science*. Gellius appears in the work as a pedant, of no independent judgment, giving himself completely to his work; but, so far as the material is concerned, his compilation is very valuable to us, — all the more, inasmuch as some of the authorities used and cited by him have not come down to us.

About the year 280, **Nonius Marcellus**,[2] probably from Africa, wrote a lexical work entitled, *compendiosa doctrina per literas*, which shows, to be sure, very little judgment and knowledge, but which has some value on account of its citations.

About the year 400, a similar compilation to that of Gellius was prepared by **Macrobius Theodosius**,[3] in his 7 books *Saturnalia*.[4] He made a liberal use of Gellius' work, and discussed the most widely-separated subjects, in particular the peculiarities of Virgil. Moreover, we have a commentary by Macrobius on Cicero's *Somnium Scipionis*,[5] which is thus preserved to us.

Martianus Capella,[6] from Madaura in Africa, a countryman of Apuleius and related to him in style, wrote about the year 430 an encyclopædic work, partly in prose, and partly in verse, after the model of Varro. He made, moreover, free use of Varro as an authority for the content of his work. After describing, in Books I and II, the wedding of Mercury

---

[1] So called, because the work was begun in Attica during the long winter nights. [2] T. ii. 314.

[3] He filled high offices, and, in his later years, probably became a Christian. T. ii. 452.

[4] The name comes from the fact that the form chosen for the work is that of a conversation held during the Saturnalia.

[5] From *de repub. VI*. [6] T. ii. 464.

and Philologia, he treats, in Books III-IX, of the seven artes liberales,—grammar, dialectics, rhetoric (the trivium of the Middle Ages), geometry, arithmetic, astronomy, and music (the quadrivium). The work was very frequently used in the Middle Ages as a school-book.

2. **Writers of text-books and commentaries** (commentarii): **Terentius Scaurus,**[1] author (under Hadrian) of a *Latin Grammar* and a *treatise on poetry*, besides several *commentarii*; only the work *de orthographia* is extant; **C. Sulpicius Apollinaris**[2] of Carthage, teacher of Gellius, and writer of *quæstiones epistolicæ*; **Helenius Acro,**[3] who wrote about the year 200, *commentaries on Terence, Horace, and Persius*; on the other hand, the collection of scholia on Horace, bearing Acro's name, is from the seventh century; **Pomponius Porphyrio** (about 200-250), writer of still extant *scholia on Horace*; **Plotius Sacerdos,**[4] writer (under Diocletian) of an extant *ars grammatica*, together with a treatise on metre; **Terentianus**[5] (Maurus), from Mauretania, likewise under Diocletian, who wrote an elementary book, *de literis, syllabis, metris*, of which the portion devoted to metre has been preserved;[6] **Iuba**[7] (about 300), probably from Africa, writer of an elementary *book on metre*, which was much used by later writers; **Marius Victorinus**[8] (about 350), writer of an extant *treatise on metre*, also of *commentaries on the Pauline Epistles*; **Ælius Donatus**[9] (about 350), writer of a *grammar*, and a *commentary on Terence*,—both extant, the commentary, however, not in its original form; **Flavius Charisius**[10] (about

---

[1] T. ii. 224; C. 463.   [3] T. ii. 278.   [5] T. ii. 327.
[2] T. ii. 235; C. 467.   [4] T. ii. 326.
[6] In describing the different metres, he always employs the metre of which he is treating.
[7] T. ii. 291.   [8] T. ii. 360.   [9] T. ii. 364.   [10] T. ii. 378.

380), writer of a *grammar*, a part of which is extant; **Diomedes**, who wrote in the same period, and often covered the same ground as Charisius; **Servius Honoratus**[1] (about 390), writer of a *commentary on Virgil*,—very valuable in subject-matter; **Priscianus**[2] (about 500), writer of *institutiones grammaticæ*, in 18 books, a most complete grammatical treatise, which, in connection with Donatus, Diomedes, and Charisius, was in universal use in the Middle Ages, and exercised the greatest influence on the treatment of grammatical subjects.

In the department of **Geography**, may be mentioned a geographical, historical compilation (*Collectanea rerum memorabilium*), written with little taste by the grammarian **C. Iulius Solinus**,[3] in the middle of the third century, — a work which, in the portion devoted to geography, was chiefly dependent upon the *Naturalis Historia* of Pliny; also, a *Cosmography*, from the seventh century, ascribed to a certain **Æthicus Ister**;[4] moreover, other unimportant writings. Of special worth are the *Itineraria*,[5] or guide-books for travellers on land and sea, which originated in the fourth century; moreover, the two *catalogues of the regiones of Rome*, the *Notitia*,[6] and the *Curiosum Urbis Romæ*; finally, the *maps*,[7] one of which, made in the time of Alexander Severus, served as a basis for the tabula Peutingeriana, a traveller's map of the Roman Empire, prepared at Colmar in 1265. It was named after its former owner, the learned Augsburg councillor, Conrad Peutinger, and is now in the Court Library in Vienna.

Astronomy, or rather **astrology**, found a zealous follower in the Sicilian rhetorician, **Firmicus Maternus**,[8]

---

[1] T. ii. 413. [3] T. ii. 312. [5] T. ii. 366. [7] T. ii. 78.
[2] T. ii. 535. [4] T. ii. 576. [6] T. ii. 368. [8] T. i. 71, ii. 353.

who, in the time of Constantine the Great, inspired by a holy zeal, wrote 8 books *Mathesios*, from the standpoint of the Neo-Platonic superstition. This pagan Firmicus Maternus must not be confounded with a contemporary Christian Firmicus Maternus, who addressed to the sons of Constantine the Great a work *de errore profanarum religionum*, urging them on to the annihilation of heathendom. The greater part of this work is extant.

Important for **Military Science** is the *Epitome rei militaris* of **Flavius Vegetius**,[1] a setting forth of Roman military science, written about the year 390. Book I treats of the levying and training of recruits; II, of military discipline; III, of war itself; IV, of the art of siege, in particular.

In **Medicine**, may be mentioned a *dispensatory* (de medicamentis), written under Theodosius I, and bearing the name of a certain **Marcellus Empiricus**;[2] but especially the two works of **Cælius Aurelianus**[3] of Numidia, one, a treatise on chronic and acute diseases,[4] and the other a medical catechism.[5] Moreover, in the fifth century and afterwards, many medical writings were translated from the Greek.

The partly-extant work on **Agriculture** written by **Gargilius Martialis**,[6] who lived in the third century, belongs also to medicine, so far as it contains the art of healing animals and other medical references. Much was transferred from this work into that of **Palladius Rutilius**[7] (fourth century) consisting of 14 books relating to agriculture.

---

[1] T. i. 75, ii. 416.   [2] T. ii. 420.   [3] T. ii. 488.
[4] Tardarum et celerum, or chronicarum et acutarum passionum.
[5] Medicinales responsiones.
[6] T. ii. 294.   [7] T. ii. 365.

e. — Patristic Literature.

Among the authors who wrote in the immediate interest of the Christian Church, for the defense and justification of Christianity against Paganism, and for the establishment and development of Christian doctrine and form of government, — the so-called Church Fathers,[1] — the following are worthy of special mention: —

Minucius Felix,[2] a Roman advocate, wrote, at the close of the second century, the dialogue *Octavius*, in which the superiority of Christianity to Paganism is shown, especially in relation to morals and civilization. The work is written in a scholarly tone, reminding one of Cicero and Seneca, and in a comparatively natural style.

Q. Septimius Florens Tertullianus[3] (150–230) of Carthage, was a rhetorician and an advocate in Rome, and afterwards a presbyter in Carthage. He was a montanist, and an original, fiery spirit, seeking to grasp the divine in concrete form, an ascetic enthusiast and a keen dialectician. His language was full of character, but arbitrary and peculiar. Among his numerous writings the *Apologeticus* of the year 199 is of special worth. **Thascius Cæcilius Cyprianus,**[4] bishop of Carthage, martyred in 258, is important in the history of church government on account of his work *de unitate ecclesiæ*. **Arnobius**,[5] of Sicca in Numidia, wrote, about 295, 7 books *adversus nationes* (heathen), in declamatory, uneven language, and without a deep understanding of Christianity.

---

[1] T. ii. 207, 338.
[2] T. ii. 272; Holden's Octavius of M. Felix: Introd.; Schaff: Hist. of Christian Church, i. 525.
[3] T. ii. 275; Woodham's Apology of Tertullian: Introd.; Schaff, i. 512.
[4] T. ii. 299; Schaff, i. 519.   [5] T. ii. 329; Schaff, i. 527.

On the other hand, **Lactantius Firmianus**[1] (under Diocletian), a rhetorician in Nicomedia, and afterwards teacher of Crispus, son of Constantine the Great, is regarded as the Christian Cicero, so far as style is concerned. His writings, among them, especially, *institutionum divinarum libri VII*, exhibit an intimate acquaintance with the best classical writers and poets, and a cultivated, tolerant mind.

A powerful champion of the glory of the church was **Ambrosius**,[2] who died as bishop of Milan in 398. He was more important on account of his personal character than on account of his writings. He took a prominent part in advancing church music, was a writer of rhymed *hymns*[3] in iambic dimeters, but not of the later so-called Ambrosian Hymn, "Te Deum laudamus."

An extremely learned and copious writer was **Hieronymus**[4] of Stridon in Dalmatia (336-420), "the disputator and dialectician of the contending church," at the same time intimately acquainted with classical literature and a connoisseur in Hebrew. The most important of his works is the *Latin translation of the Bible*,[5] the foundation of the still received Vulgate.

By far the most prominent of all the Church Fathers was **Aurelius Augustinus**,[6] who was born at Tagasta in Numidia, 354 A.D., was bishop of Hippo Regius, and died in 430. He was an extremely versatile spirit, who united in himself the most varied gifts and talents. He was of the greatest importance for the development of ecclesiastical dogma. Among his many writings the 22 books *de civitate*

---

[1] T. ii. 330; Schaff, iii. 955.
[2] T. ii. 423; Schaff, iii. 961.
[3] Trench, 86; Schaff, iii. 590.
[4] T. ii. 425; Schaff, iii. 967.
[5] His translation of the Bible is in its way a masterpiece. T. ii. 427; Schaff, iii. 972.
[6] T. ii. 441; Schaff, iii. 989.

Dei[1] are most worthy of mention, a historical, philosophical work, which exhibits a thorough knowledge of Roman and Greek literature, and has preserved to us much from both. His *confessiones* is his most popular work.[2]

Among the popes may be named **Leo the Great**[3] (Leo I), pope 440-461, the founder of the greatness of the papal throne, and a strenuous defender of church unity. His writings are partly *sermones* (delivered on festival occasions), partly *epistulæ*, written in comparatively pure style. **Gregory the Great**[4] (Gregory I), pope 590-604, also deserves mention. He was a man of monastic tendency, disdaining grammatical rules and worldly science. His most important works are his *epistles* and *hymns*. He was likewise active in the furtherance of church music.

---

[1] The grandest and most characteristic work of later Roman literature. Schlegel, 138; Schaff, iii. 1010.

[2] Schaff, iii. 1005; Shedd's Introd. to Am. Ed.

[3] T. ii. 480; Schaff, ii. 314.   [4] T. ii. 569.

SURVEY OF ROMAN LITERATURE.

POETRY.

	Drama.	Epos.	Lyric Poetry.
FIRST PERIOD. TO 240 B.C.	Fescennini. Satura (in the oldest sense).	Form: versus Saturnius. Songs on Historical Subjects. Neniæ. Carmina triumphalia. Epitaphs.	Carmen Arvalium, Carmen Saliare, and other Sacred Songs.
SECOND PERIOD. 240–70 B.C. 200 100	Atellanae. Fabula prætexta. Fabula togata. Fabula palliata. Liv. Andronicus. Cn. Nævius. Q. Ennius. **T. Maccius Plautus.** Statius Cæcilius. **P. Terentius,** Titinius, Lavinius. **M. Pacuvius.** L. Accius. T. Quinct. Atta. **L. Afranius.** Novius. L. Pomponius.	Liv. Andronicus. Nævius. Ennius. L. Accius. Lucilius, satura = Satire.	

PROSE.

	History.	Oratory.	Special Sciences.		
			Jurisprudence.	Philology and Archaeology.	Agriculture.
FIRST PERIOD. To 240 B.C.	Earliest Treaties. Commentarii and Libri magistratuum (L. lintei). Fasti. Annales pontificum. Private chronicles. Laudationes funebres.	Ap. Claud. Caecus.	Leges regiae. Commentarii regum. Libri pontificum. Commentarii pontif. Fasti. Leges XII tabularum. Ius Flavianum.		
SECOND PERIOD. 240–70 B.C. 200	(Q. Fab. Pictor. L. Cinc. Alimentus. C. Acil. Glabrio. A. Postum. Albinus.) M. Porcius Cato cens. Cassius Hemina. C. Sempr. Tuditanus. L. Calp. Frugi. L. Cael. Antipater.	Cato. C. Sulpic. Galba. C. Gracchus.	S. Aelius Paetus. Cato.		Cato. (Mago.)
100	P. Rutil. Rufus, Q. Lutat. Catulus, Sempr. Asellio, L. Corn. Sisenna, Val. Antias, L. Corn. Sulla, Claudius Quadrigarius, C. Licinius Macer.	M. Antonius. L. Crassus. Q. Hortensius. Rhet. ad Herennium.	P. Muc. Scaevola. Q. Muc. Scaevola.	L. Aelius Stilo.	

POETRY.

THIRD PERIOD. 70 B.C.–14 A.D.	Drama.	Epos.	Lyric Poetry.	Idyll.	Satire.	Epistle.
	Mimus. Dec. Laberius. Publil. Syrus.	Lucretius. Cicero.	C. Licinius Calvus. Catullus.			
30		P. Terentius. Varro Atacinus.				
		L. Varius. Pedo Albinovanus.				
	Pantomimus. (Pylades, Bathyllus.)	Vergilius. Rabirius.	Horatius.	Vergilius.	Varro. Horatius.	Horatius.
		Gratius Faliscus.	Corn. Gallus. Tibullus.			
		Manilius.	Propertius.			
1		Ovidius.	Ovidius.			Ovidius.

PROSE.

THIRD PERIOD.

THIRD PERIOD. 70 B.C.–14 A.D.	History.	Oratory.	Philosophy.	Jurisprudence.	Special Sciences.			
					Philology and Archaeology.	Agriculture.	Mathematics and Architecture.	Geography.
	Acta senatus. Acta populi.	C. Memmius.						
	Cicero. Q. Ælius Tubero.	**Cicero.** M. Cælius.	Cicero.	S. Sulpic. Rufus.	P. Nigid. Figulus.			
	T. Pompon. Atticus.	C. Curio.						
	Iulius Cæsar. A. Hirtius. **Nepos. Sallustius.**	Cæsar. M. Cælius Rufus.		M. Ter. Varro.	Cæsar. Varro.	Varro.		
30	Asinius Pollio.	Asinius Pollio.	Q. Sextii Nigri.	A. Ofilius. C. Trebat. Testa.				
	Augustus. M. Vips. Agrippa.	M. Val. Messala.		M. Antist. Labeo. C. Ateius Capito.				Agrippa.
	Livius.						Vitr. Pollio.	
1		Cassius Severus.			M. Verrius Fl. Iul. Hyginus.			Hyginus.

POETRY.

FOURTH PERIOD. 14–117 A.D.	Drama.	Epos.	Lyric Poetry.	Satire.	Fable.	Epigram.
	Pomponius Secundus.	Germanicus.			Phaedrus.	
	Curiatius Maternus.	Nero.	Caesius Bassus.			
	Lucanus. Seneca. (Octavia).	**Lucanus.** (Lucilius Iunior.) Val. Flaccus. Silius Italicus. Papinius Statius.	**Statius.** Arruntius Stella. Sulpicia.	**Persius.** Seneca.		
100				Iuvenalis.		**Martialis.**

FOURTH PERIOD.

PROSE.

FOURTH PERIOD. 14-117 A.D.	History.	Oratory.	Philosophy.	Special Sciences.					
				Jurisprudence.	Philology and Archaeology.	Mathematics and Architecture.	Agriculture.	Geography and Natural Science.	Medicine.	Military Science.
	Cremut. Cordus; Tiberius; Claudius; Agrippina minor; Aufidius Bassus. **Velleius Paterculus.** Valer. Maximus.	Seneca maior.		Masur. Sabinus. Sempr. Proculus.	Claudius.				Corn. Celsus.	
	Curtius Rufus.		Seneca minor.	Cass. Longinus.	Remmius Palaemo.		Columella.	Pompon. Mela. Seneca minor.		
	Vespasianus. Plinius maior. Cluvius Rufus.				Valer. Probus. Asconius Pedianus. Plinius maior. Aemil. Asper.	Frontinus.		Plinius maior.	Scribon. Largus.	Plinius maior. Frontinus.
	Fabius Rusticus. **Corn. Tacitus.**	Tacitus. Quintilianus. Plinius minor.			Flav. Caper. Vel. Longus.	Hyginus.				Hyginus.

ROMAN LITERATURE.

FIFTH PERIOD. AFTER 117 A.D.	POETRY			PROSE		
	Epos.	Lyric Poetry.	Fable.	History.	Oratory.	Philosophy.
200		Pervigil. Veneris.		Suetonius. Florus. L. Ampelius. Granius Licinianus.	**Corn. Fronto.** Apuleius.	Apuleius. (M. Aurelius.)
300	Nemesianus. Vettius Iuvencus.			Marius Maximus. Scriptores historiae Augustae.		
400	Festus Avienus. Aurel. Prudentius. Ausonius. **Claudius Claudianus.**			**Ammian. Marcellinus.** Eutropius. Aurelius Victor.	Symmachus.	
	Rutilius Namatianus. Apollinaris Sidonius. Dracontius.		Avianus.	Notitia dignitatum. Sulpicius Severus. Orosius.		
500	Venantius Fortunatus.			Cassiodorius. Gildas. Gregorius Turon.		Boëtius.

FIFTH PERIOD.

PROSE.

FIFTH PER.	Jurisprudence.	Philology and Archæology.	Special Sciences — Mathematics and Astronomy.	Agriculture.	Geography and Natural Science.	Medicine.	Military Science.	Patristic Literature.
afters 117 A.D.	Salvius Iulianus. Sex. Pomponius. Gaius.	Sulpic. Apollinaris. Terent. Scaurus. A. Gellius. Hesamus Acro.						Minucius Felix.
200	Æmil. Papinianus. Dom. Ulpianus. Iulius Paulus.	Pomp. Porphyrio.						**Tertullianus.** **Cyprianus.**
300	Her. Modestinus. Cord. Gregor.	Nonius Marcellus. Plotius Sacerdos. Terentian. Maurus. Iuba. Marius Victorinus. Æl. Donatus. Flav. Charisius. Diomedes. Servius Honoratus.	Firmicus Maternus.	Gargilius Martialis.	Tabula Peuting. Iul. Solinus.			Arnobius. Lactantius.
	Cod. Hermogen. Fragm. Vaticana.				Notitia Urb. Romæ. Curiosum Urb. Romæ.			
400	Cod. Theodos.	Macrobius.		Palladius Rutilius.		Marcellus Empiricus	Flavius Vegetius.	**Ambrosius.** **Hieronymus. Augustinus.**
		Martianus Capella.				Caelius Aurelianus.		
500	**Corpus iuris** Tribonianus.	**Priscianus.**			Æthicus Ister.			Leo I. Gregorius I.

INDEX.

A.

Accius, 23.
Acilius Glabrio, 27.
Acro, see Helenius.
Acta senatus, 82.
Acta populi, 82.
Ælius Donatus, 131.
Ælius Lampridius, 124.
Ælius Pætus, 31.
Ælius Spartianus, 124.
Ælius Stilo, 32.
Ælius Tubero, 72.
Æmilius Asper, 111.
Æmilius Papinianus, 128.
Æmilius Probus, 76.
Æsopus, the tragedian, 38.
Æthicus Ister, 132.
Ætna, 92.
Afranius, 22.
African latinity, 115.
Agriculture, 33, 113, 133.
Agrippa, see Vipsanius.
Agrippina minor, 99.
Albius Tibullus, 56.
Ambrosius, 121, 135.
Ammianus Marcellinus, 125.
Ampelius, 124.
Annæus Lucanus, 90.
Annæus Seneca, rhetorician, 106.
Annæus Seneca, philosopher, 89.
    Tragedies, 89.
    Satire, 93.
    Philosophical writings and epistles, 108.
Annales maximi, 12.
Annales pontificum, 12.

Annalists, 26, 27, 28.
Anthropology, 112.
Antistius Labeo, 84, 110.
Antonius, M., orator, 30.
Apollinaris Sidonius, 117.
Apuleius, 120, 121.
Archæology, 32, 84, 129.
Archaic prose, 25, 26.
Architecture, 83, 84.
Arithmetic, 83, 131.
Arnobius, 134.
Arruntius Stella, 97.
Artes liberales, 83, 131.
Artistic Drama, 16, 17, 18.
Asconius Pedianus, 111.
Asinius Pollio, 59, 79, 81.
Astrology, 132.
Astronomy, 33, 112, 131, 132
Ateius Capito, 84, 110.
Atellanæ, 10, 16.
Atticus, see Pomponius.
Aufidius Bassus, 99.
Augustinus, 135.
Augustus, 78, 98.
Aurelius Cassiodorius, 126.
Aurelius Symmachus, 120.
Aurelius Victor, 124.
Ausonius, see Magnus.
Avianus, 119.
Avienus, see Festus.

B.

Bathyllus, 39.
Boëtius, see Manlius.
Book-trade, 34, 37, 87.
Botany, 112.

147

C.

Cæcilius Cyprianus, 134.
Cælius Antipater, 28.
Cælius Aurelianus, 133.
Cælius Rufus, 59.
Cæsar, see Iulius.
Cæsius Bassus, 92, 97.
Calidius, 59.
Calpurnius Piso Frugi, 28.
Carmen, 8.
Carmen Arvalium, see Sacred songs.
Carmen Saliare, see Sacred songs.
Carmina Triumphalia, 9.
Cassiodorius, see Aurelius.
Cassius Hemina, 28.
Cassius Longinus, 110.
Cassius Severus, 59.
Catullus, see Valerius.
Celsus, see Cornelius.
Charisius, see Flavius.
Chronicles, 13, 26.
Church Fathers, 134.
Cicero, see Tullius.
Cincius Alimentus, 27.
Claudius Cæcus, 13.
Claudius Claudianus, 117.
Claudius, Imperator, 98, 110.
Claudius Quadrigarius, 29.
Cluvius Rufus, 99.
Codex Gregorianus, 128.
Codex Hermogenianus, 128.
Codex Iustinianeus, 128.
Codex Theodosianus, 128.
Columella, see Moderatus.
Comedy, 17, 22.
Commentarii magistratuum, 12.
Commentarii pontificum, 12.
Commentarii regum, 12.
Contaminare, 18.
Cornelius Celsus, 113.
Cornelius Fronto, 119.
Cornelius Gallus, 53.
Cornelius Nepos, 75.
Cornelius Sisenna, 28.
Cornelius Sulla, 28.
Cornelius Tacitus, 101.
Cornificius, 31.

Corpus iuris, 128.
Crassus, L., orator, 30.
Cremutius Cordus, 98.
Curiatius Maternus, 89.
Curio, 59.
Curiosum urbis Romæ, 132.
Curtius Rufus, 100.
Cyprianus, see Cæcilius.

D.

Dialectics, 83, 131.
Didactic poetry, 37, 39, 40, 92, 116, 118.
Digesta, 129.
Diomedes, 132.
Domestic economy, 33.
Domitius Ulpianus, 128.
Donatus, see Ælius.
Dracontius, 118.
Drama, 9, 16, 38, 89.

E.

Edictum perpetuum, 127.
Elegy, 52.
Encyclopædic literature, 82, 112, 129.
Ennius, 14, 15, 18, 22, 24.
Epic poetry, 8, 23, 37, 39, 88, 90, 116, 117.
Epicureanism, 65.
Epigram, 97, 116, 117.
Epistle (poetical), 39, 40, 48, 116, 117.
Epistle (prose), 68, 107, 110, 120.
Epitaphs, 9.
Erotic poetry, 52, 53, 56, 57.
Eutropius, 125.
Exodium, 10, 16.

F.

Fable, 96, 119.
Fabius Pictor, 26.
Fabius Quintilianus, 106.
Fabius Rusticus, 99.
Fabula palliata, 17.
Fabula prætexta, 22.
Fabula rhinthonica, 19.
Fabula togata, 22.
Fasti, 12.
Fescennini, 10.

INDEX.

Festus Avienus, 118.
Festus, see Pompeius.
Firmicus Maternus, 132.
Flavius Caper, 111.
Flavius Charisius, 131.
Flavius Merobaudes, 117.
Flavius Vegetius, 133.
Flavius Vopiscus, 124.
Florus, 123.
Fragmenta Vaticana, 128.
Frontinus, see Iulius.
Fronto, see Cornelius.

G.

Gaius, 127.
Gargilius Martialis, 133.
Gellius, 129.
Genus Asiaticum, 30, 58.
Genus Atticum, 31, 58.
Genus Rhodium, 58.
Geography, 33, 84, 85, 112, 132.
Geometry, 83, 131.
Germanicus, 92.
Gildas, 126.
Gracchus, C., 30.
Grammar, see Philology.
Granius Licinianus, 124.
Gratius Faliscus, 45.
Greek influence, 2, 7, 14, 30, 34, 64.
Gregorius I (Magnus), 136.
Gregorius Turonensis, 126.

H.

Helenius Acro, 131.
Herennius Modestinus, 128.
Hexameter, 24.
Hieronymus, 135.
Hirtius, 75.
Historical songs, 8
History, 16, 26, 72, 88, 98, 122.
Horatius, 46, 51.
    Satires, 47.
    Epistles, 48.
    Odes, 49.
    Epodes, 50.
Horace and Virgil, 51.

Hortensius, 30.
Hyginus, 85.
Hyginus (Surveyor), 111.
Hymns to the dead, 9.

I.

Idyll, 39, 40, 42, 116, 117.
Iguvinæ tabulæ, 9.
Institutiones, 129.
Iordanis, 126.
Italic language and dialects, 3.
Itineraria, 132.
Iuba, 131.
Iulius Cæsar, 59, 73.
Iulius Capitolinus, 124
Iulius Frontinus, 111.
Iulius Paulus, 128.
Iulius Solinus, 132.
Iunius Iuvenalis, 93.
Ius Ælianum, 32.
Ius Flavianum, 13. 31.
Ius Papirianum, 12.
Iustinus, 82.
Iuvencus, see Vettius.

L.

Laberius, Dec., 39.
Lactantius Firmianus, 135.
Latin language, 3.
Laudationes funebres, 13.
Law, 16, 31, 83, 110, 115, 127, 130.
Leges XII tabularum, 13.
Leges regiae, 12.
Leo I (Magnus), 136.
Libraries, 35.
Libri lintei, 12.
Libri magistratuum, 12.
Libri pontificum, 12.
Licinius Calvus, 52.
Licinius Macer, 29.
Livius Andronicus, 18, 22, 23.
Livius, T., 79.
Lucanus, 90.
Lucilius, C., 25.
Lucilius Junior, 92
Lucretius, 40.
Ludicrum Oscum, 10.

Luscius Lavinius, 21.
Lutatius Catullus, 28.
Lyric poetry, 37, 49, 50, 52, 96, 116.

M.

Maccius Plautus, 19.
Macrobius, 130.
Mæcenas, 41, 46.
Magnus Ausonius, 116.
Mago, 33.
Manilius, 45.
Manlius Boëtius, 121.
Marcellus Empiricus, 133.
Marcus Aurelius, 115.
Marius Maximus, 124.
Marius Victorinus, 131.
Martialis, see Valerius.
Martianus Capella, 130.
Masurius Sabinus, 110.
Mathematics, 33, 111, 122.
Medicine, 83, 112, 113, 133.
Mela, see Pomponius.
Memmius, 59.
Merobaudes, see Flavius.
Military writings, 111, 113, 133.
Mime, 38, 89.
Mineralogy, 112.
Minucius Felix, 134.
Moderatus Columella, 113.
Monumentum Ancyranum, 71.
Mucius Scævola, P. and Q., 32.
Music, 83, 131.

N.

Nævius, 18, 22, 24.
Namatianus, see Rutilius.
Nemesianus, 118.
Neniæ, see Hymns to the dead.
Nepos, see Cornelius.
Nero, 90.
New Academy, 65.
Nigidius Figulus, 84.
Nonius Marcellus, 130.
Notitia dignitatum, 127.
Notitia Urbis Romæ, 132.
Novellæ, 129.
Novius, 16.

O.

Octavia, prætexta, 89.
Ofilius, 84.
Oratory, 16, 29, 88, 105, 119.
Orosius, 126.
Ovidius, 53.

P.

Pacuvius, 22.
Palladius Rutilius, 133.
Palliata, 17.
Pandects, 129.
Panegyric Literature, 115.
Pantomime, 39, 89.
Papinianus, see Æmilius.
Papinius Statius, 91, 97.
Patristic literature, 115, 134.
Pedo Albinovanus, 40.
Persius Flaccus, 93.
Pervigilium Veneris, 116.
Petronius Arbiter, 94.
Peutingeriana tabula, 132.
Phædrus, 96.
Philology, 32, 83, 84, 110, 122, 129, 131.
Philosophy, 64, 108, 113, 121, 130.
Plautus, see Maccius.
Plinius maior, 99, 112.
Plinius minor, 107.
Plotius Sacerdos, 131.
Pompeius Festus, 84.
Pompeius Trogus, 82.
Pomponius, L., 16.
Pomponius Atticus, 69, 72.
Pomponius Mela, 112.
Pomponius Porphyrio, 131.
Pomponius Secundus, 89.
Pomponius Sextus, Jurist, 127.
Popular Epos, 8, 23.
Porcius Cato censorius, 27, 30, 32, 33.
Porphyrio, see Pomponius.
Postumius Albinus, 27.
Prætexta, 22.
Priscianus, 132.
Proculus, see Sempronius.
Propertius, 57.
Provincial literature, 37, 114.

INDEX. 151

Prudentius Clemens, 116.
Publilius Syrus, 39.
Pylades, 39.

Q.

Quinctius Atta, 22.
Quintilianus, see Fabius.

R.

Rabirius, 40.
Recitationes, 37.
Remmius Palæmo, 111.
Rhetoric, 50, 58, 88, 105, 113, 114, 119, 131.
Rhetorica ad Herennium, 31.
Ritual precepts, 9.
Roscius, comedian, 38.
Rutilius Namatianus, 118.
Rutilius Rufus, 28.

S.

Sabinus, see Masurius.
Sacred songs, 9.
Sallustius, 76.
Salvius Iulianus, 127.
Satire, 25, 37, 40, 45, 47, 92, 97.
Satura, 10, 16, 25.
Satura Menippea, 45.
Saturnius versus, 8.
Scribonius Largus, 113.
Scriptores historiæ Augustæ, 124.
Sempronius Asellio, 28.
Sempronius Proculus, 110.
Sempronius Tuditanus, 28.
Seneca, rhetorician, see Annæus.
Seneca, philosopher, see Annæus.
Septimius Florens Tertullianus, 134.
Servius Honoratus, 132.
Sextii Nigri, 65.
Sidonius, see Apollinaris.
Silius Italicus, 91.
Sisenna, 28.
Solinus, see Iulius.
Stage, the, in Rome, 10.
Statius Cæcilius, 21.
Statius, see Papinius.
Stoicism, 65, 109.

Suetonius, 122.
Sulla, see Cornelius.
Sulpicia, 97.
Sulpicius Apollinaris, 131.
Sulpicius Galba, 30.
Sulpicius Rufus, 84.
Sulpicius Severus, 126.
Surveyors, 167.
Symmachus, see Aurelius.

T.

Tacitus, see Cornelius.
Terentianus, 131.
Terentius, P , 20.
Terentius Scaurus, 131.
Terentius Varro, polyhistor, 45, 82
Terentius Varro Atacinus, 42.
Tertullianus, see Septimius.
Theatre in Rome, 17.
Tiberius, 98.
Tibullus, see Albius.
Titinius 22.
Togata, 22.
Tragedy, 22.
Treaties, 11.
Trebatius Testa, 84.
Trebellius Pollio, 124.
Tribonianus, 128.
Triumph, songs of, 9.
Tucca, 44.
Tullius Cicero, 59.
    Epic Poems, 40.
    Orations, 62.
    Rhetorical writings, 68.
    Philosophical works, 64.
    Letters, 68.
    Historical works, 72.
    Character, 71.

V (U).

Valerius Antias, 29.
Valerius Catullus, 52.
Valerius Flaccus, 91.
Valerius Martialis, 97.
Valerius Maximus, 100.
Valerius Messala, 59, 79
Valerius Probus, 111.

Varius, L., 40, 44.
Varro, see Terentius.
Vegetius, see Flavius.
Velius Longus, 117.
Velleius Paterculus, 99.
Venantius Fortunatus, 118.
Vergilius, 41, 51.
Verrius Flaccus, 84.
Vespasianus, 99, 111.

Vettius Aquilius Iuvencus, 117.
Victorinus, see Marius.
Vipsanius Agrippa, 79, 85.
Vitruvius Pollio, 85.
Ulpianus, see Domitius.
Volcacius Gallicanus, 124.

Z.

Zoölogy, 112.

www.ingramcontent.com/pod-product-compliance
Lightning Source LLC
Chambersburg PA
CBHW031448160426
43195CB00010BB/897